BARRON'S

PAINLESS

Writing

Jeffrey Strausser

Third Edition

Published by Kaplan, Inc., d/b/a Barron's Educational Series
750 Third Avenue
New York, NY 10017
www.barronseduc.com

ISBN: 978-1-4380-0784-7

Library of Congress Control No. 2015954491

Date of Manufacture: November 2017

9 8 7 6 5

Kaplan, Inc., d/b/a Barron's Educational Series print books are
available at special quantity discounts to use for sales promotions,
employee premiums, or educational purposes. For more information
or to purchase books, please call the Simon & Schuster special sales
department at 866-506-1949.

CONTENTS

To Beth, Katie, and Matthew

INTRODUCTION

What this book will do for you

Many students admit that their writing detracts from their hard work, rather than complements it. They realize that when they write with an uninteresting and mechanical style, they compete at a disadvantage. Unfortunately, these students sometimes become confused about how to improve their faulty writing style. Does your writing hurt you? If you think that it does, can you improve your writing? Absolutely! Can you improve your writing quickly? Absolutely! However, you must know how to go about it.

Developing a good writing style is similar to learning to play a sport or a musical instrument because writing well also requires mastering specific techniques. Did you ever notice how great athletes and musicians make what they are doing look natural? Yet we know athletes and musicians must learn their specific skills. Similar to sports and music, writing improvement comes from first separating the techniques, then studying the techniques, and finally, permanently incorporating them into your writing style. This book presents powerful and easily applied techniques to make your writing clear, interesting, and concise. Employing these techniques will immediately transform your writing style so that you can write better with less time and effort—and your grades will improve as your writing improves.

The good news is that you will not need to memorize endless lists of vocabulary words, or diagram sentences, or conjugate verbs before you can make these techniques work for you. These focused techniques will require only a small amount of time to master.

This book explains nine Painless Techniques that will dramatically improve your writing. Each technique has its own chapter that describes and demonstrates the technique through straightforward examples. Practice makes permanent; each chapter contains writing exercises to help you make these techniques a permanent part of your writing style. Finally, for the Internet surfers, each chapter contains sections where you can surf through the Internet to read additional information about topics discussed in the chapter. It is not necessary to refer to these sites, as each Painless Technique is concisely but thoroughly explained within the pages of the chapter. However, if surfing through the ocean of cyberspace is fun for you, just look for the *Surf's up* box and check out the web pages listed there.

Does dramatically improving your writing and improving your grades appeal to you? If so, grab the reins and take control of your writing. It is never too late to develop a clear, interesting, and concise writing style. The sooner you begin, the sooner it will happen. It's painless!

Web Addresses Change!

You should be aware that addresses on the World Wide Web are constantly changing. While every attempt has been made to provide you with the most current addresses available, the nature of the Internet makes it virtually impossible to keep abreast of the many changes that seem to occur on a daily basis.

If you should come across a web address (URL) that no longer appears to be valid, either because the site no longer exists or because the address has changed, don't panic. Simply do a key word search on the subject matter in question. For example, if you are interested in finding out more about prepositional phrases and the particular address appears to be invalid, do a search for various words related to prepositional phrases. These are the key words. A key word search for this topic might include, for example, noun phrases. If an initial key word search provides too many potential sites, you can always narrow the number of choices by doing a second key word search that will limit your original search to only those sites that contain the terms from both your first and second searches.

WARNING: Not every response to your search will match your criteria, and some sites may contain adult material. If you are ever in doubt, check with someone who can help you.

CHAPTER ONE

Clean Up
Preposition Clutter

PREPOSITION OVERUSE RUINS YOUR STYLE

Have you ever read something where the writer used too many words to describe what was happening or to describe something? Remember growing increasingly frustrated until you said, "Enough, already!" and started skimming, or worse yet, you just quit reading? Many times, a writer using multiword, vague prepositional phrases rather than one-word descriptive adjectives or prepositions causes wordy writing because he or she uses many words when only a few are needed. Unfortunately, the problems do not stop there because many students substitute prepositional phrases throughout their writing where verbs would have been the better choice. This writing fault leaves them with a passage that is now not only wordy, but also dull. This wordiness and dullness causes readers to skim, and once they begin skimming, they are not going to fully appreciate the work that you put into your assignment.

Look at some of your writing. Be honest. Is it wordy . . . dull . . . hard to understand? Maybe you are writing with too many wordy and vague prepositional phrases. If you are, don't worry! This common writing fault can be easily corrected. All you have to do is use the Painless Technique presented in this chapter and you will soon be

ELIMINATING UNNECESSARY PREPOSITIONAL PHRASES.

Don't overdo it!

Do not try to eliminate all prepositions from your writing because prepositions and prepositional phrases provide your reader with additional information about the nouns and verbs in the sentences you have written. The problem is that many writers overuse them because they think this is the only way to provide information. However, you will soon learn that is not the case. Overusing prepositions is a common fault, which, left unattended, develops into a bad habit that leads to wordy and dull writing. We certainly don't want to do that! Therefore, eliminate all *unnecessary* prepositions and their accompanying wordy baggage. The first Painless Technique will help you eliminate this dull baggage from your writing. Let's start by stating this first technique.

Painless Technique

#1: MAKE YOUR WRITING CLEARER AND MORE INTERESTING BY ELIMINATING UNNECESSARY PREPOSITIONAL PHRASES.

IDENTIFYING PREPOSITIONS

Make sure you can identify prepositions and their phrases

A *preposition* is a word used to link a noun to a sentence, and, in so doing, relates the noun to either another noun or a verb. The English language contains many words that can function as prepositions. Below are words that commonly function as prepositions:

by	because	at
under	during	before
for	from	behind
near	like	beside
about	over	between
on	in	into
against	until	of
to	across	off
with	above	without
next	toward	such
inside	outside	

A *prepositional phrase* consists of a preposition and a noun or a pronoun acting as the preposition's object. Within this phrase, the preposition depicts a relationship to the noun. Some prepositional phrases are shown below.

on the beach	*off* the cuff
near the desk	*after* it
against the wind	*across* the continent
from the beginning	*toward* the end
under the table	*with* whom

Surf's up...

If you want to check out the ocean of information available on identifying prepositions, a great site is

www.chompchomp.com/terms/preposition.htm

Now that we can identify prepositions and their accompanying phrases, we should ask

HOW MANY PREPOSITIONS ARE TOO MANY?

Unfortunately, there is no easy rule to tell you whether you have overloaded your writing with prepositions. Nevertheless, if your sentences contain only a few verbs, especially verbs in the passive voice, and many prepositions, your report or essay is probably wordy and confusing. (In Chapter Three we talk more about what happens to your writing when you use the passive voice.) Alternatively, if you are a numbers type person, here is a reasonable rule of thumb. If your writing contains 20 percent to 25 percent prepositions, you probably have used too many prepositions.

Too many prepositions

Unnecessary prepositions and their wordy baggage, as well as passive voice sentences, riddle the following writing excerpt. Notice how difficult it is to stay interested in this excerpt. Imagine several pages of this!

Exploring Mars

At this point in time, Mars is the target of NASA (National Aeronautics and Space Administration). Because of its closeness to Earth, Mars is being studied by scientists for the purposes of a future mission. In a manner similar to the earlier study of the Moon by scientists, a probe is planned to be sent by NASA to within the immediate vicinity of the planet, with a view toward collecting data with respect to the atmosphere of the planet. NASA plans to send in excess of one dozen of these probes during the course of the next five years.

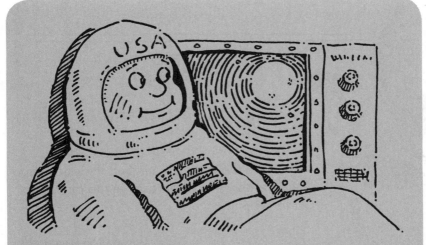

From the point of view of some nonscientists, the proposed expenditure of billions of dollars for the purpose of studying an inhospitable planet such as Mars appears to be a waste of money. In their opinion, at this point in time, our own country is in need of support in the financial area, particularly with regard to the improvement of the infrastructure.

At this point in time, from our point of view, by saying the choice in this matter is to either explore Mars and work on no other concerns does not properly frame the question under consideration. Our country is in control of vast financial resources. By virtue of this, in the event that our lawmakers can work together, they should be able to devise a budget during the course of each year that will take into consideration both our desire to explore Mars in relation to our need to update our country's infrastructure.

This writing excerpt is an extreme example of preposition overuse. The following exercise will work on identifying prepositions and their accompanying prepositional phrases.

BRAIN TICKLERS
Set # 1

Exploring Mars contains 255 words, of which 61 are prepositions.

Underline the prepositions and their accompanying prepositional phrases in the *Exploring Mars* writing excerpt.

(Answers are on page 34.)

The following is a revised version of *Exploring Mars* without the clutter of unneeded prepositions and their accompanying phrases. Although this excerpt is only 126 words long (and contains four prepositions), it provides the same information as the longer excerpt while being so much easier to read. Don't worry if you may not have been able to rewrite the excerpt like this. The rest of this chapter will show you how.

Because it is relatively close to Earth, NASA (National Aeronautics and Space Administration) is currently targeting Mars for future missions. Similar to the earlier Moon study, NASA is planning a near-vicinity probe to collect atmospheric samples. They are planning a dozen Mars probes over the next five years.

Some nonscientists feel we are wasting billions of dollars to study an inhospitable planet, and this money could be better spent improving our infrastructure. However, saying the choice is either explore Mars or improve our infrastructure does not properly frame the question. Our country controls vast financial resources. If lawmakers can work together, they should be able to devise a budget annually that considers both our desire to explore Mars and our need to update our infrastructure.

Beware of long sentences containing many prepositions

Take another look at *Exploring Mars*, and this time notice the preposition-filled next-to-last sentence of the first paragraph. The writer makes the sentence even more difficult to read by making it a long sentence laced with unnecessary prepositions and their wordy baggage.

THE PREPOSITION-FILLED LONG SENTENCE

In a manner similar to the earlier study of the Moon by scientists, a probe is planned to be sent by NASA to within the immediate vicinity of the planet, with a view toward collecting data with respect to the atmosphere of the planet.

The good writer strives to be clear, concise, and interesting. Writing long sentences filled with prepositions is a sure way to lose your reader's interest.

The real test is in the reading

The original *Exploring Mars* writing excerpt had a 24% preposition-to-total words ratio. By contrast, the rewritten version had a 3% preposition-to–total words ratio. What an improvement! Nevertheless, the preposition-to-total words ratio aside, the real test to determine whether you have used too many prepositions is in the reading. If you find yourself reading a dull passage, or skimming over words, perhaps the writing is suffering from preposition overload. As you become more aware of this common,

and curable, writing fault, it will become second nature to you to look at your writing and ask yourself

<u>WILL ELIMINATING SOME PREPOSITIONS</u>
<u>IMPROVE THIS WRITING PIECE?</u>

If you suspect prepositions often clutter your writing, apply the technique of this chapter by using the following five-step process to reduce preposition clutter.

FIVE STEPS TO ELIMINATING UNNECESSARY PREPOSITIONS

Step One: Examine your writing for compound prepositional phrases. Once identified, replace each compound prepositional phrase with a simple preposition.

Step Two: Where possible, convert candidate prepositional phrases to participles.

Step Three: Where possible, convert candidate prepositional phrases to adverbs.

Step Four: Where possible, convert candidate prepositional phrases to adjectives.

Step Five: Write selected passive voice sentences in the active voice.

With Step One, we'll start by tackling one of the greatest causes of clutter and dullness: the compound prepositional phrase.

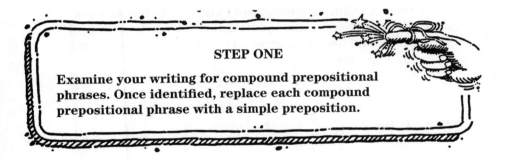

STEP ONE

Examine your writing for compound prepositional phrases. Once identified, replace each compound prepositional phrase with a simple preposition.

Identify and eliminate compound prepositional phrases

A *compound prepositional phrase* is a series of prepositional phrases that act like a single preposition. Many writers ignore simple, powerful prepositions such as *on* and *of*. Instead, they select wordy compound prepositional phrases because they think doing so makes the writing style more sophisticated. Actually, the opposite is true. Wordy compound prepositional phrases make your writing clunky and dull. Selecting the proper verb and prepositions will keep your reader interested.

Compound prepositional phrases are nothing but clutter

Below are some common compound prepositional phrases. As you read them, notice how they are formed.

with regard to = with regard + to
with respect to = with respect + to
in reference to = in reference + to
in connection with = in connection + with
in favor of = for

A compound prepositional phrase begins with a complete prepositional phrase. Unfortunately, it is a prepositional phrase that cannot stand alone, so it must combine forces with another preposition just to link the noun to the sentence. Consequently, this creates an additional prepositional phrase, making the sentence even more wordy. What is the solution to eliminating this type of wordiness? Convert compound prepositions to simpler prepositions, or eliminate the entire compound prepositional phrase. Below are some examples demonstrating how some wordy compound prepositions can be reduced to single-word prepositions or eliminated.

Convert the compound prepositions to simple prepositions or eliminate them

FIRST ATTEMPT
In connection with any sport, much practice is necessary.

BETTER
With any sport, much practice is necessary.

By deleting the prepositional phrase, *in connection with*, we have rid ourselves of an unnecessary preposition and wordy baggage.

FIRST ATTEMPT
Paulo is *in favor of* going to the park.

BETTER
Paulo is *for* going to the park.

The wordy compound prepositional phrase, *in favor of,* was eliminated and replaced with the single-word preposition, *for.*

FIRST ATTEMPT
These procedures are required *in accordance with* school policy.

BETTER
These procedures are required *by* school policy.

BETTER STILL
School policy requires these procedures.

The wordy compound prepositional phrase, *in accordance with,* is replaced by the single-word preposition, *by.* Notice, however, that the sentence is still written in the passive voice. If you're a little confused about understanding the difference between active and passive voice, hang on and we'll discuss the difference shortly. For a detailed discussion, refer to Chapter Three. The last sentence uses the active voice and eliminates the preposition, *by.* Notice that the word count drops from nine words in the first sentence to five words in the active, direct last sentence.

FIRST ATTEMPT
I am writing *in reference to* the free ticket offer.

BETTER
I am writing *about* the free ticket offer.

Here, the compound prepositional phrase, *in reference to,* is replaced with the one-word preposition, *about.*

The following are some common compound prepositional phrases and their simpler counterparts. Learn to recognize and replace the wordy compound prepositional phrase with its simple preposition.

Compound Prepositional Phrase	Simple Preposition
by means of	by
by reason of	because of
by virtue of	by, under
during the course of	during
for the purposes of	for, under
from the point of view of	from, for
in accordance with	by, under
in a manner similar to	like
in excess of	more than, over
in favor of	for
in relation to	about, concerning
in terms of	in
in the nature of	like
in the immediate vicinity of	near
in close proximity to	near
on the basis of	by, from
with reference to	about, concerning
with regard to	about, concerning
with respect to	about, concerning

BRAIN TICKLERS
Set # 2

First, identify and underline the compound prepositional phrases in each of the following sentences. Next, rewrite the sentences using concise, simple prepositions. The number in parentheses at the end of each sentence denotes the number of words in the sentence. Notice how many words you eliminate by replacing the compound prepositional phrase with a simple preposition.

1. The Smiths live in the immediate vicinity of our school. (10)

2. By virtue of winning the most games during the season, our team earned the home court advantage. (17)

3. I live in close proximity to you. (7)

4. During the course of our conversation, we decided not to spend in excess of ten dollars. (16)

5. He called me in reference to the new class that was forming. (12)

6. He ate in excess of six doughnuts. (7)

7. I am in favor of taking another class trip. (9)

8. Anna journeyed to Phoenix by means of car. (8)

9. During the course of the class, I fell asleep. (9)

10. I have a question in relation to my final social studies grade. (12)

(Answers are on pages 34–35.)

Use participles to help eliminate unnecessary prepositions

After you have eliminated all wordy compound prepositional phrases, you will have done much to improve your writing. However, there are still four more steps in this technique to help rid your writing of wordiness and dullness caused by preposition overuse. Step Two encourages you to examine your writing for prepositional phrases that can be converted into verb forms, known as participle*s*.

A *participle* is a verbal form of a word, having the qualities of both verb and adjective. For this reason, we also refer to a participle as a *verbal adjective*. Notice how the participles below help convey a sense of action.

> *Smiling* but silent, John left the room.
> *Crying*, the girls ran from the dance.

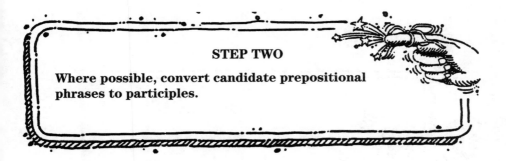

STEP TWO

Where possible, convert candidate prepositional phrases to participles.

FIRST ATTEMPT

In the attempt to write a concise essay, he omitted important facts.

BETTER

Attempting to write a concise essay, he omitted important facts.

The above example shows how you can eliminate the three-word prepositional phrase, *in the attempt* to, with the one-word participle, *attempting*. The following example shows how you can eliminate two wordy prepositional phrases with one stroke.

FIRST ATTEMPT

In the fear of failure, he sought help with his English homework.

BETTER

Fearing failure, he sought help with his English homework.

Notice that not only does this step eliminate unnecessary words, but it also gives the revised sentence a greater sense of action.

FIRST ATTEMPT

To the neglect of himself, Juan gave me his food.

BETTER

Neglecting himself, Juan gave me his food.

Here we have a compound preposition, *to the neglect of*. The sentence can be improved by replacing this compound preposition with the participle, *neglecting*.

BRAIN TICKLERS
Set # 3

First, identify the simple prepositional phrase or compound prepositional phrase in each of the following sentences. Next, rewrite each sentence by converting the prepositional phrase to a participle form. Notice how your new sentence portrays more action and is less wordy. Remember that the numbers in parentheses refer to the word count in each sentence. Take notice of the word count in your new sentence.

1. In the regard of my grade, the teacher was against changing it. (12)

2. With a sense of doom, she began crying. (8)

3. In his desire to do well academically, John quit playing video games. (12)

4. In a race against time, Sally stayed up all night working. (11)

5. With an eye on the storm clouds, the family unpacked the picnic basket. (13)

6. Without much concern, Sandy walked alone. (6)

7. In need of money, the students called home. (8)

8. In his hurry to paint the birdhouse, John spilled the paint. (11)

9. With a lack of common sense, the boys raced the train. (11)

10. With his lack of manners, Edgar embarrassed everyone watching him. (10)

11. With the hope of landing a movie part, the young actor studied his lines. (14)

12. With a taste of victory, the runner sped up. (9)

(Answers are on pages 35–36.)

Squeeze action out of adverbs

After you have transformed the appropriate prepositional phrases into verb forms, try to convert, where possible, the remaining prepositions into adverbs. An *adverb* is a word that describes a verb, an adjective, or another adverb, and tells where, when, how, how often or how long, or how much.

Below are some examples of commonly used adverbs:

> The team won *easily*.
> I *hardly* knew the teacher.
> The cyclist hit the ground *hard*.
> He arrived *late* for the play rehearsal.

When you replace prepositions with adverbs, your writing conveys a greater sense of action.

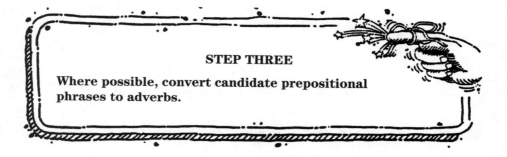

STEP THREE

Where possible, convert candidate prepositional phrases to adverbs.

FIRST ATTEMPT

The writer's novels were *of critical acclaim*.

BETTER

The writer's novels were *critically acclaimed*.

Notice how changing the prepositional phrase, *of critical acclaim*, to an adverb phrase, *critically acclaimed*, creates a greater sense of action in the second sentence.

FIRST ATTEMPT

The patient's symptoms were *under a close watch*.

BETTER

The patient's symptoms were *closely watched*.

In this example, the prepositional phrase, *under a close watch*, transforms to an adverb phrase, *closely watched*.

BRAIN TICKLERS
Set # 4

Identify the prepositional phrase in each of the following sentences, and then rewrite each sentence by converting the prepositional phrase to an adverb. Notice how the new sentence portrays more action with fewer words.

1. The President was under heavy guard.

2. Roberto was under the mistaken thought that he was finished.

3. The celebrity's actions were under close observation.

4. The politician's speech was under sharp criticism.

5. The broken elevator was in rapid descent.

(Answers are on pages 36–37.)

Take advantage of the power of adjectives

An *adjective* is a word that describes a noun or pronoun and tells which one, what kind, or how many. Adjectives help your readers visualize your facts, characters, and point of view. The next step of the technique requires that, where possible, you change the remaining unnecessary prepositions and their accompanying words to adjectives.

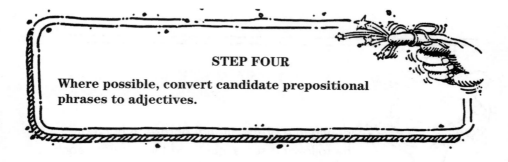

STEP FOUR

Where possible, convert candidate prepositional phrases to adjectives.

FIRST ATTEMPT

It is the nature *of humans* to admire beauty.

BETTER

It is *human* nature to admire beauty.

Notice how changing the prepositional phrase, *of humans*, to an adjective makes the sentence read more smoothly while using fewer words.

FIRST ATTEMPT

The response *of the audience* was silence.

BETTER

The *audience's* response was silence.

Again, notice how converting the prepositional phrase to an adjective makes the sentence read more smoothly while using fewer words.

BRAIN TICKLERS
Set # 5

Begin by identifying and underlining the prepositional phrase in each of the following sentences. Once selected, rewrite each sentence
by converting the prepositional phrase to an
adjective so that the revised sentence reads
more smoothly and contains fewer words.

1. The loss of time will never be regained. (8)

2. John's manner of speaking bored the
   audience. (7)

3. The quarterback was the leader of the
   team. (8)

4. Nocturnal animals avoid the light of day.
   (7)

5. The famous adventurer now craved a life of calm. (9)

6. What to wear was the problem of the day. (9)

7. Living a life of luxury had become second nature. (9)

8. The response of the class to the teacher's joke was many groans. (12)

(Answers are on page 37.)

Be active, not passive

After you have eliminated all compound prepositional phrases and, where possible, transformed prepositions and their associated words to verbs, adverbs, or adjectives, check your sentences to be sure they are written in the active voice, rather than the passive voice. Using unnecessary prepositions will often lead to passive voice sentences, which will make your writing even more dull. This happens because the subject in a passive voice sentence, rather than performing the action, is acted upon. When this happens, your writing loses directness and energy. Let's look at a better alternative to the passive voice: the active voice.

What is the active voice? Simply stated, when a sentence is written in the active voice, the subject of the sentence is the person or thing performing the action. This sentence structure creates a greater sense of action, and it does so with fewer words. For further explanation of the active versus the passive voice, refer to Chapter Three, which illustrates how to identify and transform passive voice sentences into active voice sentences. Chapter Three also discusses other problems besides wordiness created by passive voice writing.

An easy way to determine whether a sentence is in the passive voice is to ask yourself, "Who or what is performing the action?" Once you have identified the actor, make that person or thing the subject of your sentence, and then complement the subject with a verb that describes the action.

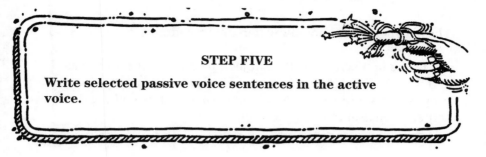

STEP FIVE

Write selected passive voice sentences in the active voice.

FIRST ATTEMPT

The exam scores were tabulated *by the teacher*.

BETTER

The *teacher* tabulated the exam scores.

In the first sentence, the subject (*exam scores*) was acted upon. This structure tells us the author has written the sentence in the passive voice. The revised sentence takes the noun contained in the prepositional phrase of the first sentence and converts it to the subject. In the revised active voice sentence, the subject, *teacher*, performs the action. Notice how the revised sentence eliminates the prepositional phrase, *by the teacher*, and how it clearly conveys who is performing what action.

FIRST ATTEMPT

The baseball card was purchased *by the collector*.

BETTER

The *collector* purchased the baseball card.

In the first sentence, the subject, *baseball card*, was acted upon. As in the example above, this structure tells us the sentence is in the passive voice. The revised sentence makes the subject, *collector*, perform the action. Notice how the new sentence eliminates the prepositional phrase of the original sentence and more clearly conveys the action.

FIRST ATTEMPT

Personal freedoms were not allowed *under the old regime*.

BETTER

The old regime did not allow personal freedoms.

In the first sentence, the subject, *personal freedoms*, was acted upon. The revised sentence eliminates the unnecessary prepositional phrase, *under the old regime*, thus making the sentence clearer and more direct.

BRAIN TICKLERS
Set # 6

Identify the prepositional phrase in the following sentences that helps create the passive voice. Next, eliminate the unnecessary prepositional phrase and rewrite the sentences in the active voice. Notice how the sentences are more direct, as well as less wordy. The number in the parentheses at the end of the sentence is the number of words in the sentence. Use it to compare the number of words in your new sentence to the original passive voice sentence.

1. The teacher's instructions were misunderstood by the students. (8)

2. His success was resented by his teammates. (7)

3. The grocery store was operated under new management. (8)

4. The grounds were observed by means of hidden cameras. (9)

5. The last four games were lost by the team. (9)

6.   The unusual plants were studied by the scientists. (8)

7.   The touchdown pass was caught by the speedy receiver. (9)

8.   The dance troupe was started by a world-renowned dancer. (10)

9.   Their desire for adventure was tempered by the rough seas. (10)

(Answers are on pages 37–38.)

This five-step process will rid your writing of most unnecessary prepositions. Extreme preposition overuse may require changing the entire paragraph structure to apply the five-step process. For instance, you may need to chop a long sentence into two or three sentences, or convert several offending simple sentences into a concise compound sentence.

APPLYING THE FIVE-STEP PROCESS

By virtue of learning better writing, you provide yourself a skill of high value. It is of importance that students in the middle schools and in the high schools realize that writers will be needed by the education and by the business communities. In the present, both sectors have expressed disappointment in the writing skills of those employed. Consequently, people who write well are in demand with employers in the nation.

This paragraph overuses prepositions. The 71-word paragraph contains 15 prepositions yielding a preposition-to-total word ratio of 20 percent. The ratio aside, this is clearly dull reading! Let's rewrite this paragraph using this first technique's five-step process. The technique involves taking each sentence and working through each of the steps until we eliminate the unnecessary preposition(s) and their accompanying wordy baggage. Our goal is to finish with a passage that is less wordy and conveys a greater sense of action.

Beginning with the first sentence:

FIRST ATTEMPT

By virtue of learning better writing, you provide yourself a skill of high value.

First, *by virtue of* is a compound prepositional phrase that you can replace with the simple preposition, *by*. (Step One). Next, *of high value* is a cluttering prepositional phrase that you can clean up by changing it to an adjective (Step Four). Now our first sentence reads:

BETTER

By learning better writing, you provide yourself a high-value skill.

Moving to the second sentence:

FIRST ATTEMPT

It is *of importance* that students in middle schools and in the high schools realize that writers will be needed *by* the education and by the business communities.

The prepositional phrase, *of importance*, can be converted to the one-word adjective, *important* (Step Four). Next, the two prepositional phrases, *in the middle schools* and *in the high schools*, can also be converted to one-word adjectives, *middle school* and *high school* (Step Four). Moreover, the sentence is in the wordy passive voice and should be rewritten into the active voice (Step Five). Let's include our Step Four changes here and create a new second sentence.

BETTER

It is important that middle school and high school students realize that the education and business communities will need writers.

Next, sentence three:

FIRST ATTEMPT

In the present, both *sectors* have expressed disappointment *in the writing skills of those employed*.

The prepositional phrase, *in the present*, can be replaced with the adverb, *presently* (Step Three). Next, we can combine the prepositional phrases, *in the writing skills* and *of those employed*, into the phrase, *their employees' writing skills*. Our new third sentence reads:

BETTER

Presently, both sectors have expressed disappointment in their employees' writing skills.

Now, on to the last sentence:

FIRST ATTEMPT

Consequently, people who write well are in demand with employers in the nation.

We spot the compound prepositional phrase, *in demand with*, and replace it with the participle, *demanding* (Step Two) when we rewrite the sentence in the active voice (Step Five). The prepositional phrase, *in the nation*, adds nothing to the sentence and can be eliminated (Step One). Using these three steps, the sentence now reads:

BETTER

Consequently, employers are demanding people who can write well.

Now we are ready for the rewritten paragraph.

> By learning better writing, you provide yourself a high-value skill. It is important that middle school and high school students realize that the education and business communities will need writers. Presently, both sectors have expressed disappointment in their employees' writing skills. Consequently, employers are demanding people who can write well.

Our new excerpt conveys the same information, not only more clearly and forcefully, but also more concisely. The rewritten paragraph contains only 50 words, a 30 percent word reduction. The prepositions decreased from 14 to just 2.

To review, the five-step process associated with this first technique is

Step One: Examine your writing for compound prepositional phrases. Once identified, replace each compound prepositional phrase with a simple preposition.

Step Two: Where possible, convert candidate prepositional phrases to participles.

Step Three: Where possible, convert candidate prepositional phrases to adverbs.

Step Four: Where possible, convert candidate prepositional phrases to adjectives.

Step Five: Write selected passive voice sentences in the active voice.

BRAIN TICKLERS
Set # 7

Transform the following wordy paragraphs into a clear and concise excerpt. Use Painless Technique No. 1's five-step process to eliminate the paragraphs' unnecessary prepositions to make the writing flow better and reduce its wordiness.

Way, Way Out There

Pluto, a dwarf planet, and Uranus, a planet, take turns being the most distant of the major bodies of our solar system in reference to the Sun. For years, scientists were under the mistaken hypothesis that Pluto was the most distant. Scientists, in an attempt to study astronomical data, learned their hypothesis was inaccurate. Fortunately, it is of the scientists' nature to investigate all data. On the basis of the data, the astronomers learned of the fact Uranus and Pluto have intersecting orbits. In addition, during the course of their investigation, they learned much of the nature of Uranus and Pluto.

The surface of both of these bodies is known to be cold because of the lack of atmosphere and their position with reference to the Sun. It is the dream of the scientific community to learn more about Uranus and Pluto. I just hope we do not lose any lives in our attempt to realize this dream.

Should we be silent with regard to this lurking danger? Scientists of notable mention have pondered in silence this very question. Nevertheless, this question, I am of the conviction, will be answered by the public, and the community of scientists.

Refer to page 38 for a suggested revision of this excerpt.

Surf's up...

While you surf through cyberspace, you can learn more about pruning unneeded prepositional phrases out of your writing. One good site that discusses some of the facets of this chapter's Painless Technique is

www.dailywritingtips.com/5-ways-to-reduce-use-of-prepositions/

Practice makes permanent

We hope that studying the chapter and working the Brain Ticklers has made this first Painless Technique part of your everyday writing style. Remember: Good writing is a skill that will help you throughout your life. Try the following, perhaps once a week, to keep your technique sharp.

1. Using a previous writing assignment, research paper, or any other submission, examine it for preposition overuse. Pull out a paragraph or two, and use this chapter's Painless Technique to create a more concise and active excerpt.

2. Look in the editorial comment section of your newspaper and select an article written by a distinguished columnist. Notice how the writer uses simple prepositions and avoids the wordy compound prepositional phrases.

Reap your rewards

Following this technique's five-step process will make your writing clearer, more forceful, and more concise. Your readers will appreciate you for not making them slog through vague and wordy writing. They will appreciate you even more if your writing is lively and holds their interest. Sound interesting? The next chapter will explain how you can enliven your writing by using another easy-to-master technique. Let's see how it works!

BRAIN TICKLERS — THE ANSWERS

Set # 1, page 8

Exploring Mars

At this point in time, Mars is the target of NASA (National Aeronautics and Space Administration). Because of its closeness to Earth, Mars is being studied by scientists for the purposes of a future mission. In a manner similar to the earlier study of the Moon by scientists, a probe is planned to be sent by NASA to within the immediate vicinity of the planet, with a view toward collecting data with respect to the atmosphere of the planet. NASA plans to send in excess of one dozen of these probes during the course of the next five years.

From the point of view of some nonscientists, the proposed expenditure of billions of dollars for the purpose of studying an inhospitable planet such as Mars appears to be a waste of money. In their opinion, at this point in time, our own country is in need of support in the financial area, particularly with regard to the improvement of the infrastructure.

At this point in time, from our point of view, by saying the choice in this matter is to either explore Mars and work on no other concerns does not properly frame the question under consideration. Our country is in control of vast financial resources. By virtue of this, in the event that our lawmakers can work together, they should be able to devise a budget during the course of each year that will take into consideration both our desire to explore Mars in relation to our need to update our country's infrastructure.

Set # 2, pages 15–16

1. The Smiths live in the immediate vicinity of our school. (10)
   The Smiths live *near* our school. (6)

2. By virtue of winning the most games during the season, our team earned the home court advantage. (17)
   By winning the most games during the season, our team earned the home court advantage. (15)

3. I live in close proximity to you. (7)
   I live *near* you. (4)

34

4. During the course of our conversation, we decided not to spend in excess of ten dollars. (16)
   During our conversation, we decided not to spend more than ten dollars. (12)

5. He called me in reference to the new class that was forming. (12)
   He called me *about* the new class that was forming. (10)

6. He ate in excess of six doughnuts. (7)
   He ate *more* than six doughnuts. (6)

7. I am in favor of taking another class trip. (8)
   I am *for* taking another class trip. (6)

8. Anna journeyed to Phoenix by means of car. (8)
   Anna journeyed to Phoenix *by* car. (6)

9. During the course of the class, I fell asleep. (9)
   During the class, I fell asleep. (6)

10. I have a question in relation to my final social studies grade. (12)
    I have a question *about* my final social studies grade. (10)

Set # 3, pages 18–19

1. In the regard of my grade, the teacher was against changing it. (12)
   Regarding my grade, the teacher was against changing it. (9)

2. With a sense of doom, she began crying. (8)
   Sensing doom, she began crying. (5)

3. In his desire to do well academically, John quit playing video games. (12)
   Desiring to do well academically, John quit playing video games. (10)

4. In a race against time, Sally stayed up all night working. (11)
   Racing against time, Sally stayed up all night working. (9)

5. <u>With an eye on the storm clouds,</u> the family unpacked the picnic basket. (13)
Eyeing the storm clouds, the family unpacked the picnic basket. (10)

6. <u>Without much concern</u>, Sandy walked alone. (6)
Unconcerned, Sandy walked alone. (4)

7. <u>In need of money</u>, the students called home. (8)
Needing money, the students called home. (6)

8. <u>In his hurry</u> to paint the birdhouse, John spilled the paint. (11)
Hurrying to paint the birdhouse, John spilled the paint. (9)

9. <u>With a lack of common sense</u>, the boys raced the train. (11)
Lacking common sense, the boys raced the train. (8)

10. <u>With his lack of manners</u>, Edgar embarrassed everyone watching him. (9)
Lacking manners, Edgar embarrassed everyone watching him. (7)

11. <u>With the hope of landing a movie part</u>, the young actor studied his lines. (14)
Hoping to land a movie part, the young actor studied his lines. (12)

12. <u>With a taste of victory</u>, the runner sped up. (9)
Tasting victory, the runner sped up. (6)

Set # 4, page 21

1. The President was heavily guarded.

2. Roberto mistakenly thought that he was finished.

3. The celebrity's actions were closely observed.

4. The politician's speech was sharply criticized.

5. The broken elevator was rapidly descending.

Set # 5, pages 23–24

1. The loss <u>of time</u> will never be regained. (8)
   The *lost time* will never be regained. (7)
   We will never regain the lost time. (7)

2. John's manner <u>of speaking</u> bored the audience. (7)
   John's *speaking manner* bored the audience. (6)

3. The quarterback was the leader<u> of the team</u>. (8)
   The quarterback was the *team leader.* (6)

4. Nocturnal animals avoid the light <u>of day</u>. (7)
   Nocturnal animals avoid *daylight.* (4)

5. The famous adventurer now craved a <u>life of calm</u>. (9)
   The famous adventurer now craved a *calm life.* (8)

6. What to wear was the problem <u>of the day</u>. (9)
   What to wear was the *daily problem.* (7)

7. Living <u>a life of luxury</u> had become second nature. (9)
   Living a *luxurious life* had become second nature. (8)

8. The response <u>of the class</u> to the teacher's joke was many groans. (12)
   The *class's response* to the teacher's joke was many groans. (10)

Set # 6, pages 26–27

1. The teacher's instructions were misunderstood <u>by the students</u>. (8)
   The students misunderstood the teacher's instructions. (6)

2. His success was resented <u>by his teammates</u>. (7)
   His teammates resented his success. (5)

3. The grocery store was operated <u>under new management</u>. (8)
   New management operated the grocery store. (5)

4. The grounds were observed <u>by means of hidden cameras</u>. (9)
   Hidden cameras observed the grounds. (5)

5. The last four games were lost <u>by the team</u>. (9)
The team lost the last four games. (7)

6. The unusual plants were studied <u>by the scientists</u>. (8)
The scientists studied the unusual plants. (6)

7. The touchdown pass was caught <u>by the speedy receiver</u>. (9)
The speedy receiver caught the touchdown pass. (7)

8. The dance troupe was started <u>by a world-renowned dancer</u>. (10)
A world-renowned dancer started the dance troupe. (8)

9. Their desire for adventure was tempered <u>by the rough seas</u>. (10)
The rough seas tempered their desire for adventure. (8)

Set # 7, pages 31–32

Below is one possible revision of the original submission. Notice that this excerpt is clearer, more direct, and more concise (189 words compared to 148 words).

Way, Way Out There

Pluto, a dwarf planet, and Uranus, a planet, take turns being the most distant major solar system body from the Sun. For years, scientists mistakenly hypothesized that Pluto was the most distant. While studying astronomical data, scientists learned their hypothesis was inaccurate. Fortunately, it is the scientist's nature to investigate all data. Based on the data, the astronomers learned Uranus and Pluto have intersecting orbits. While investigating, they also learned much more about Uranus and Pluto.

Scientists know the surfaces of these bodies are cold because they lack atmosphere and they are far from the Sun. It is the scientific community's dream to learn more about Uranus and Pluto. I just hope we do not lose any lives attempting to realize this dream.

Should we be silent about this lurking danger? Notable scientists have silently pondered this very question. Nevertheless, I am convinced the public, not the scientific community, will answer this question.

CHAPTER TWO

Spice Up Your Writing

DULL WORDS MEAN DULL WRITING

Have you ever picked up a story or an article that you could not put down? Try to recall what riveted you to the writing. It's likely that the action made the piece come alive. Because verbs convey action, chances are the writer connected you to the writing by using lively verbs. Weak writers leave their readers unable and unwilling to identify with the page's lifeless words. If you want your writing to be something a reader cannot put down, then your next question should be

HOW DO I CONNECT READERS TO MY WRITING?

It means first getting rid of all those dull and vague verbs, and replacing them with action verbs . . . hard-hitting verbs . . . descriptive verbs.

> The boys *raced* home.
> The boys *strolled* home.
> John *glanced* at Mary.
> John *stared* at Mary.

Actions speak louder than words, unless they are action words

Is your writing lively? Rummage through some of your old writing assignments and check out the verbs that you used. Do they portray a sense of action? Do they clearly describe the characters? Just like preposition overuse, writing with dull and vague verbs is a common writing fault.

Readers will hang on your every word, but only if you provide them with something interesting on which to hang. Active and descriptive verbs provide the written handholds. Writing without these types of verbs invites readers to start skimming and possibly miss the point of your writing. Therefore, the best way to avoid this situation is to eliminate those dull and vague verbs from your writing. You can accomplish this by employing the second Painless Technique. Let's take a look at it.

Painless Technique

#2: CONNECT READERS TO YOUR WRITING WITH VIVID VERBS.

IDENTIFYING THOSE HARD-WORKING VERBS

Before we can use this chapter's technique, we first have to identify the verbs in our writing. Because parts of speech have been pounded into your heads since grade school, you should not have any problem picking them out. Just in case, however, let's have a little review.

We can classify verbs into two major groups: action verbs and linking verbs. We are most familiar with action verbs. Those are the verbs that convey the action performed by the subject. For instance,

> The student *wrote* the essay in class.
> The dog *ate* the homework.
> The cow *jumped* over the moon.

Within the action verb group is a subset group of verbs known as *helping verbs*. They are called helping verbs—you guessed it!—because they help the action verb. The most common helping verbs are conjugations of "be" and "have." Helping verbs are most often used to express a time frame for the action associated with the action verb. The two verbs together form a *verb phrase*.

We *are expecting* it to rain.

In this example, *are* is a helping verb and *expecting* is an action verb. Notice how we can use the verb phrase *are expecting* to express an action that will occur in the <u>future</u>.

We *have eaten* our dinner.

Here, *have* is a helping verb and *eaten* is an action verb. They combine to form the verb phrase *have eaten*, which expresses an action that occurred in the <u>past</u>.

Wrote, ate, and *jumped* are **action verbs** because they convey the action performed by the subject.

The other major group of verbs is the **linking verbs**. Linking verbs are quite different from action verbs. They don't express action, but rather connect or link the subject of the sentence to the other words in the sentence that describe the subject (*the subject complement*).

Juan *is* ill.
The dog *appears* nervous.
We *are* late.

Linking verbs have their place in writing, of course. However, we must be careful about overusing them, especially linking verbs known as **being verbs**. Below is a list of the being verbs:

is	are	were	being
am	was	be	been

Overusing ***being verbs*** will rob your writing of action or clarity, or both. These particular verbs are sometimes referred to as "dead verbs." You can avoid this writing pitfall by eliminating these dead verbs from your writing whenever possible. You do that by employing this chapter's technique of using vivid verbs. If you write with strong, vivid verbs, many times you can eliminate whole sentences written with dead verbs because your reader will not need the information you had to provide because your weak verbs weren't getting the job done. Sound good? Let's get started. We'll go over this technique step by step to make sure we get it down.

BRAIN TICKLERS
Set # 8

In the following paragraph, the author writes about a young lady named Claire. Underline the verbs and identify whether they are **action verbs** or **linking verbs**.

Claire

Claire walked down the crowded hallway on this first day of school. She was confident. Claire looked quickly to her left, and then to her right. Then, she walked out and joined the throng of students. She was curious. How many students saw her? Although she wanted to look around, she looked straight ahead. However, it seemed that none of her class-mates looked at her while they walked quickly to their classes. Claire was sad.

(Answers are on page 64.)

Surf's up...

Need a little more practice identifying verbs? The following is a good site to surf into for some more practice:

http://leo.stcloudstate.edu/grammar/verbsub.html

After you have identified the verbs, read *Claire* again. Were you involved with the passage's events? Did the writing excerpt tell you anything definitively about Claire, such as whether she is shy or outgoing, or whether she is pretty or plain? You cannot tell, can you? That is because the writer has not painted a vivid mental picture, so you disinterestedly sit on the sidelines. Bland writing does that to readers; consequently, bland writing penalizes student writers with lower grades. You must engage your reader into your writing's characters and action. This holds true whether you are writing a creative piece or a research paper. Let's return to the paragraph featuring Claire.

The excerpt is bland because the verbs the writer uses to describe Claire's actions are general. True, they denote actions, but the actions they convey are watch-from-a-distance actions. Consequently, the author tries to provide more information by using sentences with linking verbs. Unfortunately, he chose "being" verbs for the job, and the only thing they accomplished was to make the excerpt wordy.

You want your reader to know what is happening, to feel a certain way about what is happening, to care about what is happening. This requires peppering your writing with vivid verbs that clearly describe the action. If you do that, you will attract and keep your reader's interest.

Replace bland verbs with vivid verbs

Vivid verbs appeal to the reader's sense impressions and arouse feelings. Vivid verbs convey exactly what is happening and draw the reader into the action. Notice the physical and mental action verbs in the sample paragraph: *walked, saw, seemed,* and *look.* These verbs describe Claire's actions and state, but very superficially. After all, there is *walking* . . . and there is *WALKING.*

There is *watching* . . . and there is *WATCHING*. General verbs such as those in our writing sample, as well as others—*go*, *say*, *come*, *walk*, *run*, *think*, *know*, *get*, and *tell*—usually do not explain the passage's action well enough. What is more, we want to do more than just explain; we want to *involve* the reader with the passage. *Claire* does not involve the reader because it does little to convey the attitude and feelings of Claire and the other students, as expressed through their actions. That is the task vivid verbs perform so well. Understanding that, let's see how we can improve this excerpt.

To force ourselves to use descriptive vivid verbs, we'll first eliminate the excerpt's dead verb sentences. Refer to the earlier list of "being verbs" so you can pick out the dead verbs. The excerpt's sentences containing dead verbs are listed below:

She *was* confident.
She *was* curious.
Claire *was* sad.

Let's improve the new first sentence by replacing its bland verb with a vivid verb.

Claire *swaggered* down the crowded hallway on this first day of school.

Swaggered describes Claire's locomotion more specifically than *walked*. What do you know about Claire now? Claire has attitude. Claire wants people to notice her. Do you think she is a plain-looking girl? I doubt it. Suppose we wrote *trudging* down the hall? Would you view Claire differently? However, let's stay with the verb *swagger*, and move on to the second sentence.

She *looked* quickly to her left, and then to her right.

Although the writer realized the verb, *looked,* would have little effect on the reader, his attempt to rescue this weak, general verb by inserting a weak, general adverb, *quickly,* was unsuccessful. This is a common technique employed by writers afflicted with a bland writing style. One of the functions of an adverb is to tell the reader more about the verb. Unfortunately, an adverb helping a vague verb is usually not as effective as a single strong verb in connecting the reader to the character. Ask yourself, how rapid is *quickly*? Also, think how many times you use the word *look* in your writing. This sentence demands a single vivid verb.

She *glanced* to her left, and then to her right.

By just changing a few verbs, you can begin picturing the situation. Moving on to the next sentence:

Then, she *walked* out and *joined* the throng of students.

You should have recognized that *walk* and *join* are general verbs. We can do better; let's start by finding a vivid verb for *walk.*

Then, she *rushed* out and *joined* the throng of students.

The sentence is better, but *joined* is not doing the job for us. Let's try replacing it with a vivid verb.

Then, she *rushed* out and *merged* into the throng of students.

Moving on to the next sentence:

How many students *saw* her?

Again, *saw* is a general verb. To enliven this sentence, try using a descriptive verb. I used *noticed,* so now we have:

Claire *swaggered* down the hall. She *glanced* to her left, and then to her right. She *rushed* out and *merged* into the throng of students. How many students *noticed* her?

The paragraph is beginning to come alive as we pepper it with vivid verbs! The next sentence overuses the bland verb, *look*.

> Although she *wanted* to *look* around, she *looked* straight ahead.

Here, the author uses the weak verb, *wanted*, and the weak verb, *look*, twice. This verb selection does very little to enthuse us about what is happening to Claire. Let's try to add some life to this sentence by replacing these weak verbs with more descriptive and vivid verbs.

> Although she *longed* to *enjoy* their admiring glances, she *stared* straight ahead.

By using the descriptive verbs, *longed* and *enjoy*, we have a much clearer picture of what Claire is thinking. Furthermore, note how the descriptive verb, *stared*, helps the reader better understand Claire's situation.

> Good writers provide insight into the story's characters for their readers.

Now we are getting somewhere. Let's work on the last sentence.

> However, it *seemed* that none of her classmates *looked* at her as they *walked quickly* to their classes.

Again, the writer realizes the weakness of the verbs *seemed*, *looked*, and *walked*. He drops in the adverb, *quickly*, attempting to provide the reader with a little more insight. Predictably, the adverb reinforcement does not do enough. We can improve this sentence by replacing the bland *seemed* and *looked* with the descriptive verb, *ignore*. Similarly, we can pump life into the sentence by replacing the weak, *walked quickly*, with the single vivid verb, *raced*. Now we make a bold statement:

However, they *ignored* her as they *raced* to their classes.

We are finished revising the paragraph. Let's look at our new paragraph:

BETTER

Claire

Claire *swaggered* down the crowded hallway on this first day of school. She *glanced* to her left, and then to her right. Then, she *rushed* out and *merged* into the throng of students. How many students *noticed* her? Although she *longed* to *enjoy* their admiring glances, she *stared* straight ahead. However, they *ignored* her as they *raced* to their classes.

Compare your new paragraph to the original version.

FIRST ATTEMPT

Claire

Claire *walked* down the crowded hallway on this first day of school. She was confident. Claire *looked quickly* to her left, and then to her right. Then she *walked* out and *joined* the throng of students. She was curious. Was anyone *watching* her? Although she *wanted* to *look* around, she *looked* straight ahead. However, it seemed that none of her classmates *looked* at her while they *walked quickly* to their classes. Claire was sad.

Notice how much more you know about Claire and her actions in just five sentences. We transformed the lifeless paragraph by first ridding it of its "dead verb" sentences, and then replacing the general verbs and weak adverb/verb combinations with vivid verbs:

swaggered for *walked*
glanced for *looked quickly*
rushed for *walked*
merged for *joined*
noticed for *saw*
longed for *wanted*
enjoy for *look*
stared for *looked*
ignored for *looked*
raced for *walked quickly*

By replacing bland verbs with vivid verbs and removing the "dead word" sentences, we transformed mediocre writing into a paragraph that connected you to Claire. Furthermore, another benefit of substituting vivid verbs is that we reduced the wordiness of the excerpt. The original paragraph contained 74 words, whereas the revised paragraph contains only 60 words. That is a 20-percent word reduction! Your teachers will thank you for enlivening your writing, as well as making it more concise.

BRAIN TICKLERS
Set # 9

Rewrite the original *Claire* by first eliminating the "dead verb" sentences, and then by replacing at least half of the vague verbs with vivid verbs. However, this time, write the paragraph to portray Claire as a shy individual.

Refer to page 64 for one version of the new paragraph.

Help your readers identify with your characters

Read the following writing excerpt entitled *Joe Freeman's Spring*. Does its author let you kknow how Joe *really* feels?

FIRST ATTEMPT

Joe Freeman's Spring

It is spring and it had come to western Pennsylvania unannounced. The oaks and the maples were very colorful and even the sedate elms were changing the boring line of the rundown farmhouses and barns by showing their colors. Full of the optimism that spring brings, Joe Freeman, jobless and broke, walked down the streets of his hometown smelling the scented air of the morning. Joe was in a good mood. Today was a perfect day to open the door of opportunity.

You get a vague idea, but it's difficult to identify with Joe, isn't it? We can improve it by eliminating the "dead verb" sentences, and then replacing the weak verbs in this following paragraph with vivid verbs, so you feel more connected to Joe Freeman.

Joe Freeman's Spring

Spring had *burst* into western Pennsylvania unannounced. The oaks and the maples were *exploding* with color and even the sedate elms were *interrupting* the boring line of the rundown farmhouses and barns by *displaying* their colors. Full of the optimism that spring brings, Joe Freeman, jobless and broke, *strode* down the streets of his hometown *drinking in* the scented air of the morning. Today was a perfect day to *kick down* the door of opportunity.

OPPORTUNITY

Notice how the second paragraph used:

> *burst* instead of *come*
> *exploding* instead of *were*
> *interrupting* instead of *changing*
> *displaying* instead of *showing*
> *strode* instead of *walked*
> *drinking in* instead of *smelling*
> *kick down* instead of *open*

The vivid verbs in the improved paragraph transform vague, dull reading into clear, interesting reading. Notice how we could eliminate those useless and wordy "dead verb" sentences without losing any information.

Strong verbs create strong feelings

Weak verbs rob your story of excitement. Notice how *The General Store* doesn't exactly leave you on the edge of your seat as you read.

The General Store

The sun shone brightly in the sky; its hot summer heat made us tired and thirsty. We continued until we came to a small country store. We walked in and saw a huge German Shepherd behind the counter. The dog had an angry look in its eyes. Concerned, we turned around and went out the door. A cloud of dust formed behind us.

BRAIN TICKLERS
Set # 10

First, read and identify the weak verbs in the excerpt *The General Store*, then rewrite the excerpt using the more specific or active verbs listed below.

billowed   spun   trudged   raced
glared   parched   staggered   noticed

This is a challenging exercise. You may want to use a dictionary and work with your classmates or friends.

Refer to pages 64 and 65 for answer and a sample rewrite.

Vivid verbs will improve all types of writing

Do not confine using vivid verbs to only creative writing assignments. Examine how the vivid verbs the author selected transformed a dull social studies paragraph into an interesting one, while conveying the same information.

FIRST ATTEMPT

Technology and capital investment are *bringing* Brazil into the next millennium. As it *changes* from socialism to capitalism, the economy is *moving* some reluctant Brazilians into the next millennium, while others are *agreeing* with the sweeping changes. The stated goal of Brazil's planners is to *control* the South American continent within five years.

BETTER

Technology and capital investment are *propelling* Brazil into the next millennium. As it *progresses* from socialism to capitalism, the economy is *dragging* some reluctant Brazilians into the next millennium, while others are *embracing* the sweeping changes. The stated goal of Brazil's planners is to *dominate* the South American continent within five years.

Notice how the author substituted vivid verbs to illustrate the Brazilian economy.

> *propelling* instead of *bringing*
> *progresses* instead of *changes*
> *dragging* instead of *moving*
> *embracing* instead of *agreeing*
> *dominate* instead of *control*

As with *Joe Freeman's Spring*, the verbs are not elaborate, but they are forceful. We use forceful verbs when we speak, so why not use them when we write? Again, vivid verbs belong in

all types of writing, and you can prove this to yourself by reading some paragraphs from publications such as *Time* and *National Geographic*. *Time* is a premier news publication and *National Geographic* is a leading natural science publication. They do not fill their pages with lifeless articles. Indeed, these publications require bold, lively writing because they must interest their readers enough to read the articles. Conversely, publishing boring articles is a sure way to drive away subscribers.

Scientific research writers also need to write with colorful verbs. Doing so will hold their readers' attention. Again, the more interested the reader remains, the better chance you have of making your point.

Below is a paragraph from a report on the Moon. Notice how the author used general verbs to describe the action.

FIRST ATTEMPT

Images of the Moon *show* enormous craters across its landscape whose jagged walls *stick out* against the horizon. Millions of years' worth of debris *falling* on the satellite has *changed* its surface. However, has the landscape only been *changed* by falling debris? The flat, broad plains may be from lava *flowing* from ancient volcanoes. Volcanoes *indicate* an active subsurface, yet today, scientists *see* a quiet subsurface underneath a dead landscape. How and why was the Moon *changed*? Scientists *are looking* for the explanation to this mystery and perhaps *help* Earth from *having* the same fate.

Below is our Moon paragraph, but it is now written with vivid verbs. Notice the difference!

BETTER

> Images of the Moon *reveal* enormous craters *strewn* across its landscape whose jagged walls *jut* against the horizon. Millions of years' worth of debris *bombing* the satellite has *etched* and *pock-marked* its surface. However, has space debris *plummeting* into the surface of the Moon been the only sculptor of the landscape? The flat, broad plains *suggest* that in the early history of the Moon *surging* lava was *expelled* from ancient volcanoes. Volcanoes *demand* an active subsurface as a source of energy, yet today, scientists observe a quiet subsurface *overlain* by a dead landscape. What process *transformed* the Moon? Scientists are *striving to unlock* this mystery and perhaps *save* Earth from *suffering* the same fate.

Notice how much more interesting the second paragraph is. The information is the same as in the first passage; however, imagine slogging through a 20-page article written in the style of the first paragraph. Predictably, after a page or two, you would begin skimming the pages. Before long, you would start flipping pages, not at all interested in the information or appreciative of the hard work that went into the paper.

BRAIN TICKLERS
Set # 11

Write your own scientific, business, or technical article using vivid verbs at least half of the time.

You may want to work on this exercise with your classmates or friends. You can also use newspapers or magazines to give you ideas for your topic.

Refer to page 65 for an example article.

SELECTING ACTION VERBS

You should now be adept at identifying "dead verb" sentences as well as weak verbs and adverb/verb combinations. Try to eliminate most of the "dead verb" sentences and replace at least half of the weak verbs with action verbs. At first, many writers might find selecting an action verb a difficult task because they use them so infrequently they are not part of their vocabulary. If this is a problem for you, the following table offers some vivid verbs to substitute for commonly used general verbs. Notice that the substitutes have somewhat different meanings.

Selected General Verbs with Their Substitute Vivid Verbs

walk	talk	look	listen
stroll	chat	glance	eavesdrop
traipse	belittle	gawk	heed
ramble	debate	gaze	attend
roam	cajole	stare	detect
meander	prattle	peep	overhear

like	run	think	need
admire	scamper	meditate	covet
cherish	scramble	picture	wish
value	hustle	ruminate	desire
honor	flee	contemplate	fancy
revere	dash	imagine	crave

help	give	stop	come
encourage	impart	fetter	appear
abet	bestow	desist	emerge
support	beget	check	arise
uphold	confer	arrest	occur
back	donate	curtail	surface

tell	make	show	want
narrate	engender	exemplify	aspire
chronicle	coerce	reveal	fancy
announce	produce	divulge	yearn
urge	fabricate	proclaim	covet
deduce	erect	explain	crave

Surf's up...

If you would like more ideas about dynamic verbs, check out the following site:

www.chompchomp.com/terms/actionverb.htm

BRAIN TICKLERS
Set # 12

Use the vivid verbs listed below to rewrite the following sentences, which use weak, general verbs.

proclaimed revealed craved debated
constructed gawking eavesdropping
hustled contemplated devour

1. The bank robber showed us his place for hiding the stolen money.

2. The crew made the building in less than six months.

3. I thought about joining the circus as I walked around under the big top.

4. As Marty listened to them, Grace and Ann talked about the surprise party they were planning for him.

5. In the summertime, I eat apples by the dozen.

6. I rushed about the house as I tried to prepare for the party.

7. The boys looked at the cute girls all day.

8. The politicians spent hours talking about what was the proper course of action.

9. Jim wanted an ice cream bar all day.

10. The art exhibit showed that Picasso was the greatest artist of that era.

Refer to page 65 for some possible sentences.

Don't count on adverbs to help

We have already witnessed in *Claire* that a general adverb does not portray a strong mental image. The weak adverb/verb combination is relatively ineffective compared to the vivid verb. To illustrate, let's begin with a sentence using a weak verb to describe the action of the subject.

Edgar *asked* me to lend him some money.

This sentence does little to involve or inform the reader about Edgar's actions. You can try to invite the reader to a more active role by inserting an adverb to help the weak verb.

Edgar *angrily asked* me to lend him some money.

The sentence is improving because we understand that Edgar really wants some money. However, we can improve this sentence by inserting a strong, vivid verb.

Edgar *demanded* that I lend him some money.

Compared to the original sentence, this sentence is crisp and exact because words such as *scared, happy, sad,* or *angry* rarely suffice to show the clear feelings of their holder. Moreover, converting them to adverbs by adding *-ly* does not improve matters because the vagueness remains. The way to improve any writing assignment is to demonstrate your characters' feelings and actions with specific verbs.

BRAIN TICKLERS
Set # 13

First, identify and underline the weak or vague adverb/verb combinations in *A Man's Best Friend*, and rewrite the passage by replacing at least half of the dull adverb/verb combinations that you identified with specific, vivid verbs. For help selecting vivid or descriptive verbs, use the previous table.

A Man's Best Friend

Since it was a very nice day, we decided to slowly walk through the park. A briskly running dog crossed our path in pursuit of a rubber ball. He quickly took the ball in his mouth and swiftly walked back to his owner. We could see the dog breathing heavily as he abruptly placed the ball at the man's feet. The man roughly patted the dog's head.

(Answers and a sample rewrite are on page 66.)

Putting it all together

You should be able to spot weak verbs and weak adverb/verb combinations with an eye toward substituting vivid verbs. Use Brain Ticklers Set # 14 to put this Painless Technique to work.

BRAIN TICKLERS
Set # 14

Transform *The Near Miss* by first eliminating the "dead verb" sentences, and then replacing at least half of the general verbs and adverb/verb combinations with active verbs. If you need to, use the table on pages 57–58 to help with this review exercise.

The Near Miss

Christine went quickly down the soccer field. She was excited. She spoke loudly to her teammate Anna, "Kick the ball to me." Anna quickly looked at Christine and then kicked the ball to her friend. With the ball in front of her, Christine moved quickly ahead and then kicked the ball toward the goal. The ball hit against the side post very hard—close, but no goal. Christine was disappointed.

Refer to page 66 for a sample rewrite.

Practice makes permanent

You should be convinced that weak, general verbs rob your writing of action and specificity, and that, ultimately, your vague writing style will cost you in the grade book. By replacing weak verbs and adverb/verb combinations with vivid verbs, you will improve your writing. As always, honing your new skill and making it a permanent part of your style should be your goal. Try the following, perhaps once a day, to keep this Painless Technique sharp.

1. Using a previous writing assignment, term paper, or any other submission, examine it for weak verb and weak adverb/verb overuse. Pull out a paragraph or two, and use your new technique to make the excerpt more lively and concise.

2. After you are satisfied with your rewrite of the selected one or two paragraphs, rewrite the rest of the assignment. When you are finished, show the two versions to your teacher.

Keep your reader involved

Now that you have mastered the second Painless Technique, move on to the next chapter to learn a technique to defeat another bad writing habit that plagues many student writers.

BRAIN TICKLERS—THE ANSWERS

Set # 8, page 44

Claire

Claire <u>walked</u> (action) down the crowded hallway on her first day of school. She <u>was</u> (linking) confident. Claire <u>looked</u> (action) quickly to her left, and then to her right. Then, she <u>walked</u> (action) out and <u>joined</u> (action) the throng of students. She <u>was</u> (linking) curious. How many students <u>saw</u> (action) her? Although she <u>wanted</u> (action) to <u>look</u> (action) around, she <u>looked</u> (action) straight ahead. However, it <u>seemed</u> (linking) that none of her classmates <u>looked</u> (action) at her while they <u>walked</u> (action) quickly to their classes. Claire <u>was</u> (linking) sad.

Set # 9, page 50

Claire

Claire <u>trudged</u> down the crowded school hallway on this first day of school. She <u>glanced</u> to her left, and then to her right. Then, she <u>walked</u> out and <u>blended</u> into the throng of students. How many students <u>noticed</u> her? Although she wanted to <u>look</u> around, she kept <u>staring</u> straight ahead. She <u>hoped</u> that none of her class-mates <u>noticed</u> her as they <u>walked</u> quickly to their classes.

Set # 10, page 53

The General Store

The sun <u>shone</u> brightly in the sky; its hot summer heat <u>made</u> us tired and thirsty. We <u>continued</u> until we <u>came</u> to a small country store. We <u>walked</u> in and <u>saw</u> a huge German Shepherd behind the counter. The dog <u>had</u> an angry look in its eyes. Concerned, we <u>turned</u> around and <u>went</u> out the door. A cloud of dust <u>formed</u> behind us. (61)

The General Store

The hot summer heat *parched* our throats. We *trudged* along until we came to a small country store. We *staggered* in and *noticed* a huge German Shepherd behind the counter who *glared* at us. Frightened, we *spun* around and *raced* out the door. A cloud of dust *billowed* behind us. (48)

Set # 11, page 56

As companies in practically every industry *rush* to sell their goods and services on the Internet, life *deteriorates* for those businesses that *languish*. Internet sales sites are *proliferating* and it seems that every business will soon own one. These companies *venturing* into cyberspace must *confront* a myriad of problems before they can *reap* the benefits of e-commerce. Companies will be *challenged* and *rewarded* in proportion to how they *embrace* the Internet.

Set # 12, page 59

1. The bank robber *revealed* his place for hiding the stolen money.

2. The crew *constructed* the building in less than six months.

3. I *contemplated* joining the circus as I walked around under the big top.

4. As Marty *eavesdropped* on them, Grace and Ann talked about the surprise party they were planning for him.

5. In the summertime, I *devour* dozens of apples.

6. I *hustled* about the house as I tried to prepare for the party.

7. The boys *gawked* at the cute girls all day.

8. The politicians *debated* for hours about what was the proper course of action.

9. Jim *craved* an ice cream bar all day.

10. The art exhibit *proclaimed* that Picasso was the greatest artist of that era.

Set # 13, page 61

A Man's Best Friend

Since it was a very nice day, we decided to <u>slowly walk</u> through the park. A <u>briskly running</u> dog crossed our path in pursuit of a rubber ball. He <u>quickly took</u> the ball in his mouth and <u>swiftly walked</u> back to his owner. We could see the dog <u>breathing heavily</u> as he <u>abruptly placed</u> the ball at the man's feet. The man <u>roughly patted</u> the dog's head.

A Man's Best Friend

Since it was a very nice day, we decided to *stroll* through the park. A *speeding* dog crossed our path in pursuit of a rubber ball. He *snatched* the ball into his mouth and *trotted* back to his owner. We could see the dog *panting* as he *dropped* the ball at the man's feet. The man *rubbed* the dog's head.

Set # 14, page 62

The Near Miss

Christine *raced* down the soccer field. She *yelled* to her teammate Anna, "Kick the ball to me." Anna *glanced* at Christine and then kicked the ball to her friend. With the ball in front of her, Christine *sped* ahead and then kicked the ball toward the goal. The ball *slammed* against the side post—close, but no goal.

CHAPTER THREE

Silence the Passive Voice

THE PASSIVE VOICE ROBS
YOUR WRITING OF ENERGY

When we speak of *voice* in the context of grammar, we are talking about how the verb operates in the sentence. Thus, if the sentence's subject *performs* the action or shows the condition described by the verb, we refer to the verb as an active voice verb, and we say that the writer has used the active voice. In contrast, if the sentence's subject receives the action of the verb, then we say the verb is a passive voice verb, and the writer has used the passive voice. Try to notice this distinction in the following example sentences.

ACTIVE VOICE
The pitcher threw the baseball to the catcher.

PASSIVE VOICE
The baseball was thrown by the pitcher to the catcher.

In the active voice sentence, the subject of the sentence, *the pitcher*, is performing the action, *throwing the baseball*. Compare this with the passive voice sentence where the subject of the sentence, *the baseball*, is receiving the action, *throwing*.

Where the action is

Although passive voice is necessary at times, overusing it robs your writing of energy. The very structure of passive voice sentences makes them wordy and, well, passive. As we noticed, passive voice sentences relegate the subject of the sentence to receive the action rather than perform the action. Therefore, when you write in the passive voice, you de-emphasize the person, animal, or object performing the action. Consequently, even though you may not have meant to, you removed the action from your main character, which is exactly the opposite of what you want to do to keep your reader interested. The effect is comparable to watching a game rather than playing it.

Below are additional examples of passive voice sentences. Notice how the subject in each of the sentences (*ax, exam, application,* and *town*) is no longer the doer of the action, but the receiver of the action.

> The ax was held by the woodsman.
> The exam had already been graded by the teacher.
> The application was rejected by the selection committee because of the poor writing sample.
> The town has been overrun by rowdy football fans.

Stay active

Did you notice how the above passive voice sentences disconnect the performer from the action? Reading relies upon images, and action creates images; therefore, by transforming the unnecessary passive voice sentences into the active voice, you will

TRANSFORM YOUR WRITING FROM DULL TO VIBRANT.

This chapter will provide a technique for, first, identifying passive voice overuse, and then, transforming the offending sentences to the active voice.

Painless Technique

#3: CHANGE ALL UNNECESSARY PASSIVE VOICE SENTENCES TO ACTIVE VOICE SENTENCES.

RECOGNIZING AND CHANGING THE PASSIVE VOICE

Overusing the passive voice is one of the most common culprits in weak writing. Fortunately, you can correct this problem rather easily. First, let's learn to identify passive voice writing.

Identifying the voices

In the active voice, the subject of the sentence always performs the action or exists in a condition described by the verb. Also, in active voice sentences where there is a direct object, the direct object receives the action performed by the subject. The following are examples of sentences written in the active voice. Notice how the action stays connected to the performer of the action. This subject-verb connection energizes your writing.

ACTIVE VOICE SENTENCES

The band (subject) *played* well.

Matt (subject) *kicked* the ball (direct object) into the goal.

Katie (subject) *served* the volleyball (direct object) over the net.

The teacher (subject) *had been gone* all week.

Subjects in passive voice sentences do not perform the action described by the verb; rather, they receive the action. The performer of the action is now either stuck in a prepositional phrase or left out of the sentence completely.

PASSIVE VOICE SENTENCES

The ball (subject) *was kicked* into the goal by Matt (performer).

The volleyball (subject) *is served* over the net by Katie (performer).

The class (subject) *had been cancelled* (performer not mentioned).

(In the above sentence, the writer implies the prepositional phrase, *by the teacher.*)

After reading the above sentences, you should now know that you have spotted a passive voice sentence whenever the verb describes the action *performed on* or *done to* the subject. Stated differently,

In a passive voice sentence, the subject does not perform the action; rather, it is acted upon.

Furthermore, passive voice sentences are always built with some form of *to be* + the past participle of a verb that acts upon the subject of the sentence. The following are some additional examples of passive voice sentences.

Arthur *was selected* by Ms. Jones to be the class representative.

Arthur *was selected* to be the class representative.

The house *had been painted* by the work crew.

The house *had been painted*.

The gold medal *was won* by the figure skater.

The gold medal *was won*.

Notice the performers of the action have lost their center spotlight or are not even mentioned in these passive voice sentences. You should now realize that passive sentences disconnect the performer and the action, and the result is dull and stilted reading.

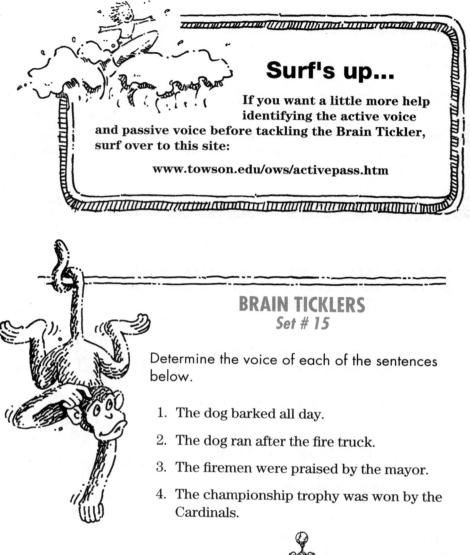

Surf's up...

If you want a little more help identifying the active voice and passive voice before tackling the Brain Tickler, surf over to this site:

www.towson.edu/ows/activepass.htm

BRAIN TICKLERS
Set # 15

Determine the voice of each of the sentences below.

1. The dog barked all day.

2. The dog ran after the fire truck.

3. The firemen were praised by the mayor.

4. The championship trophy was won by the Cardinals.

5. The girls sang loudly.

6. The sisters had argued over the car for an entire week.

7. John had been away for a long time.

8. New York was selected by the committee as the site for its annual meeting.

9. The saxophone player received an encore.

10. The secretary is answering the telephone.

11. All occurrences of the passive voice were eliminated by the student writers.

12. The violinist practiced every day.

13. John stayed after class to meet with the teacher.

14. Bob had stopped at every traffic light.

15. The compositions were returned by the teacher at the end of class.

(Answers are on pages 87–89.)

Three steps change your voice

Now that you can identify passive voice sentences, let's learn the following three-step procedure for converting them to active voice sentences. By learning this simple procedure, you will be ready to apply this chapter's Painless Technique of changing all unnecessary passive voice sentences to active voice sentences.

Step One:

Identify a passive verb sentence by looking for a verb form that consists of *both* the past participle and a form of *to be* that acts upon the subject.

For instance, look at the following sentence:

Norma Jean *was selected* by the seventh grade to present their demands. (12)

The verb, *was selected*, acts upon the sentence's subject, *Norma Jean*. Therefore, this sentence is written in the passive voice.

Once you have identified a passive voice sentence such as the one above, you are ready for Step Two.

Step Two:

Locate the person or thing in the sentence performing the action. This noun will be either part of a prepositional phrase or absent from the sentence (but implied by the writer).

In our sentence, *the seventh grade* performs the action.

Step Three:

Convert the action-performing noun or the noun that is omitted but implied to be the action performer into the subject of your revised sentence. Usually, the subject of the original sentence becomes the direct object in the active voice sentence.

Applying the three-step technique to the original sentence yields the revised sentence. The original subject, *Norma Jean*, is now the direct object.

The seventh grade selected Norma Jean to present their demands. (10)

Notice that the revised version contains fewer words than the passive voice sentence, which demonstrates that active voice sentences are not only livelier, but they are more concise.

BRAIN TICKLERS
Set # 16

Use Painless Technique No. 3's three-step process to transform the passive voice sentences of Set # 15 to active voice sentences.

(Answers are on page 89.)

WHEN THE PASSIVE VOICE IS NECESSARY

Your writing will immediately improve because you are now an expert at identifying passive voice writing and transforming it to the active voice. However, there are times, and they are rare, when the passive voice is necessary.

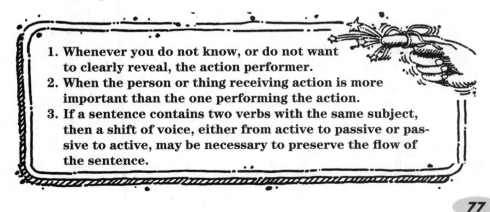

1. **Whenever you do not know, or do not want to clearly reveal, the action performer.**
2. **When the person or thing receiving action is more important than the one performing the action.**
3. **If a sentence contains two verbs with the same subject, then a shift of voice, either from active to passive or passive to active, may be necessary to preserve the flow of the sentence.**

Let's look at each of these special situations.

Special passive situation no. 1

The passive voice is necessary whenever you do not know, or do not want to clearly reveal, the action performer. The following sentences demonstrate this situation.

> Thunderstorms and hail *had been forecast* for the morning of the field trip.

In this passive voice sentence, the writer has chosen not to reveal that *meteorologists* had forecast the thunderstorms.

> Noises *were being made* all over the house.

Here, *scurrying mice* could have made the noises. However, the writer chose not to reveal this to the reader.

> The swimming meet *has been postponed*.

The writer chose not to reveal that the meet director had postponed the swimming meet.

> The day *has been ruined*.

The day may have been ruined *by thunderstorms*; only the writer knows.

BRAIN TICKLERS
Set # 17

Determine whether the following sentences are written in the active or passive voice. If the sentence is written in the passive voice, decide whether it should remain in the passive voice because the writer does not know or does not want to clearly reveal the source of the action.

1. Threats were being issued throughout the tense ordeal.

2. The summit meeting had been convened.

3. The student council meeting was convened by Bob.

4. His fate had been known.

5. His fate had been known by the fortune-teller.

6. The military secrets had been stolen.

7. The spy stole the military secrets.

8. The military secrets had been stolen by the spy.

9. Trash was being thrown all over the yard.

10. John threw trash all over the yard.

(Answers are on pages 90–91.)

Special passive situation no. 2

Passive voice verbs are also necessary when the person or thing receiving action is more important than the one performing the action.

> The Queen of England was welcomed by all.
> The class field trip was postponed.
> The Kentucky Derby had been run by hundreds of horses.

In the example passive voice sentences, the *Queen of England,* the *class field trip,* and the *Kentucky Derby* are the receivers of the action. They are more important than the performers of the action. Therefore, the passive voice is necessary to show their relative importance.

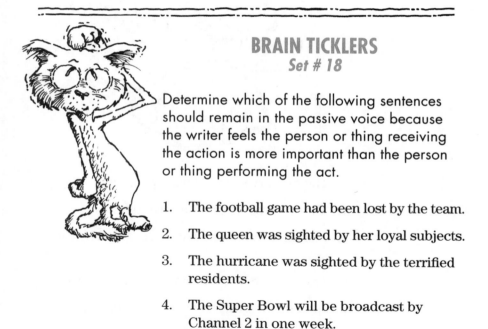

BRAIN TICKLERS
Set # 18

Determine which of the following sentences should remain in the passive voice because the writer feels the person or thing receiving the action is more important than the person or thing performing the act.

1. The football game had been lost by the team.

2. The queen was sighted by her loyal subjects.

3. The hurricane was sighted by the terrified residents.

4. The Super Bowl will be broadcast by Channel 2 in one week.

5. The president will be interviewed by the newscaster.

(Answers are on page 91.)

Special passive situation no. 3

If a sentence contains two verbs with the same subject, then a shift of voice, either from active to passive or passive to active, may be necessary to preserve the flow of the sentence.

> The Tigers *won* the championship game, and *were awarded* the Governor's Trophy.

The verbs shift from the active (*won*) to passive (*were awarded*); however, they have the same subject, *the Tigers*. Because both the verbs have the same subject, using the passive voice helps the flow of the sentence. Compare this sentence to one where using both voices creates confusion and wordiness.

> As *we gazed* at the horizon, *the sailboats were seen* against the setting sun.

Notice, the subject of the active voice verb (*gazed*) is *we*. However, switching to the passive voice (*were seen*) caused the author to shift the subject (*sailboats*). The shift from the active to the passive voice (or vice versa) in the above sentence leaves the sentence confusing and stilted because the writer shifted subjects as well. In so doing, the action flow was disrupted. Avoid changing voices if doing so causes you to change subjects as well. Notice that the above sentence can be more clearly written in the active voice.

> As *we* gazed at the horizon, *we* saw the sailboats against the setting sun.

Surf's up...

Want more information on when to use the passive voice? Check the following site:

www.writing.utoronto.ca/advice/ style-and-editing/passive-voice

BRAIN TICKLERS
Set # 19

Determine which of the following sentences should remain unchanged although they contain both passive voice and active voice verbs.

This is a difficult exercise. Carefully review the preceding material before you begin.

1. The band finished rehearsal and was given a well-deserved rest.

2. As the king surveyed his empire, treachery was plotted by his enemies.

3. Before the campers left, the wolves had been heard howling in the woods.

4. The campers ventured into the woods and were attacked by wolves.

5. The wolves ran away as the hunters were heard calling for help.

(Answers are on pages 91–92.)

PUTTING IT ALL TOGETHER

To reiterate, situations where writing in the passive voice is necessary occur infrequently. Once you determine that none of the above three situations applies, use the three-step process to reduce the unnecessary passive voice sentences in your writing.

BRAIN TICKLERS
Set # 20

Apply this chapter's Painless Technique to improve the following writing excerpt, *Anna at the Science Fair.* Use the technique's three-step process to transform the unnecessary passive voice sentences to active voice sentences. Keep in mind the special situations that require the passive voice. The number in parentheses at the end of the paragraph is the word count of the excerpt. You should also notice how your new paragraph is more concise, as well as easier to understand.

Anna at the Science Fair

Anna worked all summer on her Science Fair presentation and was rewarded for her hard work. She was selected by her school to represent it at the district Science Fair. Her science teacher was surprised by her experiment's innovation. At the Science Fair, Anna's findings were applauded by the judges as insightful. Later that day, her presentation was awarded the grand prize by the impressed judges. As she received her award, her proud parents could be seen taking photographs. The Science Fair had been a tremendous success! (87)

Refer to page 93 for a suggested rewrite.

WHAT ABOUT WRITING A SCIENTIFIC PAPER?

Good science is gathering results from objective studies and objectively reporting them. Unfortunately, some writers mistake objectivity in reporting results with the illusion of objectivity created by writing in the third person. Their logic is simple, but flawed. They correctly observe that the active voice will necessarily require an increased use of the first person—*I observed this*, or *We performed the following tests*. Unfortunately, *I* and *we* are mistakenly viewed as too subjective, and this rationale leaves the third person as the objective writer's only alternative.

The following excerpt illustrates the unfortunate result associated with writing a scientific paper in the disassociated, passive voice style.

FIRST ATTEMPT

Saturn

Observations were made by the scientists from the University of California regarding the rings of Saturn. It is the analysis and conclusion of this group that ice, frozen gasses, and rock particles comprise the rings of Saturn. Further observations will be made by the group as an understanding of the relationship between the rings of Saturn and the moons of Saturn is the goal of the group. (67)

Imagine reading several pages of that style of writing! It is difficult to become excited about their findings. In contrast, pick up any *Scientific American* magazine and read the feature articles. You will notice very little passive voice writing in them because the magazine editors and the writers want the readers to read the articles. Therefore, they communicate with their readers in a concise and direct way without sacrificing objectivity. You should do the same when you are writing a scientific paper. Do not confuse objective reporting with wordy writing.

Practice makes permanent

You should be convinced that the passive voice is the enemy of a concise and interesting writing style. By learning the Painless Technique for spotting passive voice writing, and changing it to improved active voice writing, you are well on your way to dramatically improving your writing. As always, honing your new skill and making it a permanent part of your style should be your ultimate goal. Try the following, perhaps once a week, to keep this technique sharp.

1. Using a previous writing assignment, examine it for passive voice overuse. Pull out a paragraph or two, and use your newly learned technique to change the passive voice sentences to active voice sentences.

2. Select a magazine article from a national magazine such as *Sports Illustrated* or *Time*. Try to spot passive voice use. Notice how few instances you find. Get the idea?

BRAIN TICKLERS
Set # 21

Rewrite the wordy, passive voice excerpt entitled *Saturn* so that it is concise and active. Notice how you can keep the scientific nature of the paragraph, and yet make it interesting. The number in parentheses represents the word count of the excerpt. Notice how much you have reduced the word count by rewriting the unnecessary passive voice sentences in the excerpt.

(Sample rewrite is on page 93.)

Activate your reader for a favorable reaction

This chapter's technique will reward your reader with more interesting and concise submissions, and you with better grades. Now that we have conquered the passive voice, let's examine another problem that will rob your writing of life—overusing nominalizations.

BRAIN TICKLERS—THE ANSWERS

Set # 15, pages 74–75

1. The dog barked all day. (active voice)
   This sentence is written in the active voice because the verb, *barked,* describes the action performed by the subject, *dog.*

2. The dog ran after the fire truck. (active voice)
   This sentence is written in the active voice because the verb, *ran,* describes the action performed by the sentence's subject, *dog.*

3. The firemen were praised by the mayor. (passive voice)
   This sentence is written in the passive voice because it contains a verb form of *to be* (*were*) and a past participle (*praised*) that describe the action received by the subject, *the firemen.*

4. The championship trophy was won by the Cardinals. (passive voice)
   This sentence is written in the passive voice because it contains a verb form of *to be* (*were*) and a past participle (*won*) that describe the action received by the subject, *championship trophy.*

5. The girls sang loudly. (active voice)
   This sentence is written in the active voice because the verb, *sang,* is describing the action performed by the subject, *girls.*

6. The sisters had argued over the car for an entire week. (active voice)
   This sentence is written in the active voice because the sentence's verb, *had argued,* describes the action performed by the sentence's subject, *sisters.*

7. John had been away for a long time. (active voice)
   This sentence is written in the active voice because the sentence's verb, *had been,* describes the action performed by the subject, *John.*

8. New York was selected by the committee as the site for its annual meeting. (passive voice)
The sentence is written in the passive voice because the sentence's verb, *was selected*, describes the action received by the sentence's subject, *New York*.

9. The saxophone player received an encore. (active voice)
The sentence is written in the active voice because the sentence's verb, *received*, describes the action performed by the sentence's subject, *saxophone player*.

10. The secretary is answering the telephone. (active voice)
The sentence is written in the active voice because the sentence's verb, *is answering*, describes the action performed by the sentence's subject, *secretary*.

11. All occurrences of the passive voice were eliminated by the student writers. (passive voice)
This sentence is written in the passive voice because the sentence's verb, *were eliminated*, describes the action received by the sentence's subject, *all occurrences*.

12. The violinist practiced every day. (active voice)
This sentence is written in the active voice because the sentence's verb, *practices*, describes the action performed by the subject, *violinist*.

13. John stayed after class to meet with the teacher. (active voice)
This sentence is written in the active voice because the verbs of the sentence, *stayed* and *meet*, describe the action performed by the subject of the sentence, *John*.

14. Bob had stopped at every traffic light. (active voice)
This sentence is written in the active voice because the sentence's verb, *stopped*, describes the action performed by the subject of the sentence, *Bob*.

15. The compositions were returned by the teacher at the end of class. (passive voice)
This sentence is written in the passive voice because the verb of the sentence, *were returned*, describes the action received by the subject of the sentence, *the compositions*.

Set # 16, page 77

3. The firemen were praised by the mayor.
(passive voice)
The mayor is the noun performing the action. Therefore, making *the mayor* the subject of the new sentence, the sentence rewritten in the active voice is: The mayor praised the firemen.

4. The championship trophy was won by the Cardinals.
(passive voice)
The Cardinals is the noun performing the action. Rewriting the sentence in the active voice, *the Cardinals* becomes the subject of the sentence: The Cardinals won the championship trophy.

8. New York was selected by the committee as the site for its annual meeting. (passive voice)
The committee is the action-performing noun of the sentence. To rewrite the sentence in the active voice, make *the committee* into the subject: The committee selected New York as the site for its annual meeting.

11. All occurrences of the passive voice were eliminated by the student writers. (passive voice)
The student writers is the action-performing noun in this sentence. To rewrite the sentence in the active voice, make *the student writers* the subject of the new sentence: The student writers eliminated all occurrences of the passive voice.

15. The compositions were returned by the professor at the end of class. (passive voice)
The teacher performs the action. To rewrite this sentence in the active voice, make *the teacher* the subject: The teacher returned the compositions at the end of class.

Set # 17, pages 78–79

1. Threats were being issued throughout the tense ordeal. (passive voice)
   This sentence should remain in the passive voice because the author does not want to reveal the source of the threats.

2. The summit meeting had been convened. (passive voice)
   This sentence should remain in the passive voice because the writer apparently does not feel it is important to know who convened the summit.

3. The student council meeting was convened by Bob. (passive voice)
   This passive voice sentence should be rewritten in the active voice because the writer has revealed the performer of the action (*Bob*).

4. His fate had been known. (passive voice)
   The sentence should remain in the passive voice because the author does not want to reveal who knew about the person's fate.

5. His fate had been known by the fortune-teller.
   This passive voice sentence should be rewritten in the active voice because the writer has revealed the performer of the action (*fortune-teller*).

6. The military secrets had been stolen. (passive voice)
   This sentence should remain in the passive voice because the writer apparently does not want to reveal who stole the military secrets.

7. The spy stole the military secrets. (active voice)

8. The military secrets had been stolen by the spy. (passive voice)
   This passive voice sentence should be rewritten in the active voice because the writer has revealed who stole the military secrets (*the spy*).

9. Trash was being thrown all over the yard. (passive voice)
   This sentence should remain in the passive voice because the writer apparently does not feel it is important to know who was throwing the trash.

10. John threw trash all over the yard. (active voice)

Set # 18, page 80

1. The football game had been lost by the team.
   This sentence should be rewritten in the active voice because it is not clear that the *game* is more important than the *team*.

2. The queen was sighted by her loyal subjects.
   This sentence should remain in the passive voice because the *queen* is an important person relative to the *loyal subjects* in the sentence.

3. The hurricane was sighted by the terrified residents.
   This sentence should be rewritten in the active voice because *hurricane* is not clearly more important than the *terrified residents*.

4. The Super Bowl will be broadcast by Channel 2 in one week.
   This sentence should remain in the passive voice because the *Super Bowl* is an important event relative to *Channel 2* in the sentence.

5. The president will be interviewed by the newscaster.
   This sentence should remain in the passive voice because the *president* is an important person relative to *the newscaster* in the sentence.

Set # 19, page 82

1. The band finished rehearsal and was given a well-deserved rest.
   This sentence is acceptable although it contains both an active voice verb (*finished*) and a passive voice verb (*was given*) because the writer has not shifted the sentence's subject.

2. As the king surveyed his empire, treachery was plotted by his enemies.
   This sentence is stilted because it contains an active voice verb (*surveyed*) and a passive voice verb (*was plotted*) and the writer has shifted the subject from *king* to *treachery*. A possible rewrite of the sentence is: As the king surveyed his empire, he was unaware of the treachery plotted by his enemies.

3. Before the campers left, the wolves had been heard howling in the woods.
   This sentence is stilted because it contains an active voice verb (*left*) and a passive voice verb (*had been heard*) and the writer has shifted the subject from *campers* to *wolves*. A possible rewrite of the sentence is: Before the campers left, they had heard the wolves howling in the woods.

4. The campers ventured into the woods and were attacked by wolves.
   This sentence is acceptable although it contains both an active voice verb (*ventured*) and a passive voice verb (*were attacked*) because the writer has not shifted the sentence's subject, *campers*.

5. The wolves ran away as the hunters were heard calling for help.
   This sentence is stilted because it contains an active voice verb (*ran*) and a passive voice verb (*were heard*) and the writer has shifted the subject from *wolves* to *hunters*. A possible rewrite of the sentence is: The wolves ran away when they heard the hunters calling for help.

Set # 20, pages 83–84

Anna at the Science Fair

Anna worked all summer on her Science Fair presentation and was rewarded for her hard work. Her school selected her to represent it at the district Science Fair. Her experiment's innovation surprised her science teacher. At the Science Fair, the judges applauded Anna's findings as insightful. Later that day, her presentation was awarded the grand prize by the impressed judges. As she received her award, she saw her proud parents taking photographs. The Science Fair had been a tremendous success! (80)

Set # 21, page 86

Saturn

My colleagues and I, scientists from the University of California, analyzed the rings of Saturn. We have concluded that Saturn's rings are comprised of ice, frozen gasses, and rock particles. We intend to further study Saturn's rings because we want to understand the relationship between Saturn's rings and its moons. (50)

CHAPTER FOUR

Reduce Nominalizations and Activate Your Writing

NOMINALIZATIONS EXPOSED!

Overusing nominalizations is a major writing flaw that creates an extreme case of boring, stuffy writing. Because we want to improve our writing, the first question we have to ask is: What is a nominalization?

A *nominalization* is a noun derived from a verb or an adjective. Examples of a noun deriving from a base verb include *seclusion, inference,* and *confinement.* You can spot these verb-based nouns by their suffixes: *-ent, -ence, -ant, -ency, -ancy, -ment, -tion,* and *-sion.* Similarly, adjective-based nouns derive from a base adjective. Adding the suffixes *-ent, -ant, -ful, -able* converts adjectives into nominalizations. Below are some common nominalizations created from verb and adjective bases.

Verb	Nominalization	Adjective	Nominalization
move	movement	thoughtful	thoughtfulness
excite	excitement	difficult	difficulty
withdraw	withdrawal	opulent	opulence
fail	failure	applicable	applicability
accept	acceptance	elastic	elasticity

Surf's up...

The following site will further help you spot nominalizations:

http://grammar.about.com/od/mo/g/nominalterm.htm

Unfortunately, many students burden their writing with nominalizations because they mistakenly believe this writing style is sophisticated. However, rather than leading to polished writing, overusing nominalizations creates vague, stilted writing. Whereas,

REDUCING NOMINALIZATIONS LIVENS UP YOUR WRITING.

Verbs create action, not nouns

Why does overusing nominalizations create vague and stilted writing? The answer lies in the nature of nouns. A *noun* refers to a person, place, quality, idea, or thing. By its very nature, any noun or noun form cannot convey motion or action to the reader, nor can it describe itself. As we learned in Chapter Two, crisp and interesting writing demands well-placed verbs and adjectives.

Why not just add some verbs and adjectives to the nominalizations to return action and description to the writing? Unfortunately, it is not that easy because whenever you begin inserting verbs and adjectives, wordiness, the other culprit of bad writing, shows up. There are two ways to attach nouns to sentences; the first way is with verbs, and the second way is with prepositions. The writer overusing nominalizations, therefore, must find verbs or prepositions to connect the nominalizations in the sentence. Moreover, nominalizations' word structures and their typical place in the sentence promote the use of weak, vague verbs and accompanying adverbs to buttress the weak verb. Chapter Two demonstrated the consequences of trying to help weak verbs with adverbs: more words, but no more action. Notice how we can write the sentences avoiding nominalizations and how the rewritten sentences are more active and concise. The numbers in parentheses denote the number of words in the sentence.

FIRST ATTEMPT
Bob made a *withdrawal* of money from his bank account. (10)

BETTER
Bob *withdrew* money from his bank account. (7)

FIRST ATTEMPT

You can make *application* of these techniques to your writing. (10)

BETTER

You can *apply* these techniques to your writing. (8)

FIRST ATTEMPT

The rubber band has a lot of *elasticity*. (8)
The detective is making the crime the subject of *his investigation*. (11)

BETTER

The rubber band is very *elastic*. (6)
The detective is *investigating* the crime. (6)

You can avoid stuffy writing by applying this chapter's Painless Technique. Let's take a look at it.

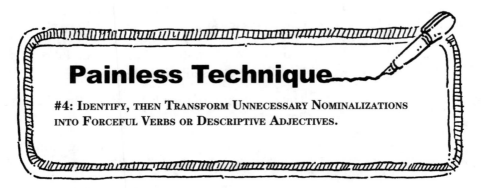

Painless Technique

#4: IDENTIFY, THEN TRANSFORM UNNECESSARY NOMINALIZATIONS INTO FORCEFUL VERBS OR DESCRIPTIVE ADJECTIVES.

Identifying nominalizations

The first part of this chapter's Painless Technique requires that you identify the offending nominalizations. If you need to, review the first part of this chapter to help you become comfortable identifying nominalizations. Once you are ready, try the following exercises that test your ability to identify nominalizations.

BRAIN TICKLERS
Set # 22

Identify and underline the nominalization in each of the following sentences, then determine the verb or adjective root along with the suffix used in creating that nominalization.

1. The senator had no recollection of his campaign promise.

2. The teacher's reaction to the news was a negative one.

3. Each candidate is under investigation before his nomination.

4. Many political prisoners have not had the benefit of representation by counsel.

5. The discussion of the class was on the field trip.

6. The mayor's office started an investigation into the council member's actions.

7. The husband and wife made a renewal of their wedding vows.

8. The newspapers launched an attack of a vicious nature at the candidate.

9. The induction of the baseball player into the Hall of Fame took place on Friday.

10. Katie's reaction was predictable.

11. Matthew made the suggestion that we stop at the campsite.

12. The editorial is a reflection of the writer's thoughts.

13. Bob's writing improvement astounded everyone.

14. The carelessness of his writing was apparent throughout the entire manuscript.

15. The general signaled for a withdrawal of his troops.

16. By your acceptance of this check, you agree to paint the house.

(Answers are on pages 116–117.)

Baggage, baggage, and more baggage

Not only does overusing nominalizations drain the life out of your
writing, but this bad writing habit
adds a lot of unnecessary words
that waste your readers' time.
The bulk of the wordy baggage
comes from prepositional phrases
that result whenever you convert
verbs and adjectives into nouns
that become the objects of the
prepositional phrases. Examine
the sentences below that contain
nominalizations.

> The boys, full <u>of *excitement*</u>,
> entered the room.

The sentence contains the nominalization, *excitement,*
which also carries with it the prepositional phrase baggage,
<u>of excitement</u>.

> The *departure* <u>of the students</u> created a chaotic scene.

This sentence contains the nominalization, *departure,* which
requires an accompanying wordy prepositional phrase, <u>of the
students,</u> to convey the writer's thoughts.

As you can see, by writing the sentences with a nominalization, the writer needed to add a prepositional phrase. Recall the
Chapter One discussion of how using too many prepositional
phrases weakens your writing. Notice how one writing flaw can
bring on another writing flaw!

More words, less action

You should now see that dullness and wordiness result when
writers overuse nominalizations. Do the following exercise to
make sure you can spot both of these problems.

BRAIN TICKLERS
Set # 23

Read the following paragraph entitled *The English Teacher*. Because it contains many nominalizations, the paragraph is wordy, yet it contains relatively few verbs. Identify the nominalizations plaguing this passage.

The English Teacher

The English teacher had little expectation that her class would attain improvement in their writing. There are few indications that what she expects should be under reconsideration. However, a discussion among the students yielded a different conclusion because they were unwilling to make an acceptance of her conclusion. It was their decision to have a discussion with the principal about the replacement of their teacher. They realized, nevertheless, that the principal would have a reluctance to accept their suggestion.

(Answers are on page 118.)

WRITING SITUATIONS THAT CREATE UNNECESSARY NOMINALIZATIONS

Eliminating unnecessary nominalizations is an easy task because it requires only that you reverse the process you used to create them. In other words, you must convert the nominalization to its verb or adjective root. The key to this technique is identifying the writing situation where this nominalization overuse usually occurs. The good news is that the overuse usually confines itself to four situations in which the weak writer typically inserts a nominalization where a verb or adjective would have been a better choice. Below are those situations where writers mistakenly use nominalizations. Once identified, a remedy is provided for converting the misused nominalizations to their adjective or verb roots.

Situation no. 1: nominalization trails a weak verb

The most common writing error involving nominalizations occurs whenever the writer inserts a nominalization after a weak verb. The weak verb didn't convey the action of the sentence well enough, so the writer mistakenly tries to help out with a noun. Now, instead of one writing problem (the weak verb), the writer adds the unnecessary nominalization. The result is a dull and wordy sentence. Observe how nominalizations trail a weak verb in the following sentences.

FIRST ATTEMPT

The commander <u>has</u> no *expectation* that the prisoners will be freed.

BETTER

The commander does not *expect* that the prisoners will be freed.

FIRST ATTEMPT

The candidates <u>have made</u> a *withdrawal* of their offers to debate on the issues.

BETTER
The candidates *withdrew* their offers to debate on the issues.

Notice that the nominalizations in each of the sentences (*expectation* and *withdrawal*) follow dull and general verbs within those sentences (*has* and *have made*). To improve the first sentence, replace the nominalization, *expectation*, with its root verb, *expect*. In the improved second sentence, the verb, *withdrew*, replaces the nominalization, *withdrawal*, and substitutes for the original weak verb, *have made*.

Situation no. 2: nominalization following an expletive construction

The next situation occurs where writers include a nominalization in an expletive construction. An **expletive construction** is a sentence that begins with such words as *there are*, *there is*, or *it is*. Because expletive constructions sometimes cause the reader to lose track of the subject, the writer drops in a nominalization to help refer the reader to the subject in the sentence. Unfortunately, doing so only makes the original sentence stilted and wordy. Changing the nominalization to a verb, and then finding a subject for the verb can easily correct this nominalization misuse situation.

FIRST ATTEMPT
It is Matt's *decision* to play the soprano saxophone in the jazz band.

BETTER
Matt *decided* to play the soprano saxophone in the jazz band.

FIRST ATTEMPT
There is no need for *acceptance* of this condition.

BETTER
You do not need to *accept* this condition.

FIRST ATTEMPT

There are *indications* that he is quitting.

BETTER

He *indicated* that he is quitting.

FIRST ATTEMPT

There has been no *movement* of the weak foundation.

BETTER

The weak foundation has not *moved*.

Notice how the rewritten sentences convey action and are concise.

Situation no. 3: nominalization is the subject of a weak verb

Using weak verbs creates yet another nominalization overuse situation, but this time the writer uses a nominalization as the subject of the empty verb.

FIRST ATTEMPT

The *decision* of the teacher is to re-grade the test.

The nominalization, *decision*, is the subject of the weak verb, *is*. Also, notice that the writer must include the prepositional phrase, *of the teacher*, to complete the sentence.

BETTER

The teacher *decided* to re-grade the test.

FIRST ATTEMPT

Our *discussion* was the test.

Here, the nominalization, *discussion*, takes on the role of subject for the weak verb, *was*.

BETTER

We *discussed* the test.

Situation no. 4: consecutive nominalizations

The final nominalization overuse situation is where the writer uses consecutive nominalizations because the writer correctly realizes that one nominalization is weak and ineffective, but then mistakenly tries to remedy the situation by adding yet another nominalization. Notice the weak verbs in the sentences containing nominalizations.

The remedy is to take advantage of the root verbs of these nominalizations. As mentioned earlier, they are more active and descriptive than the filler verbs the writer has used to connect the nominalizations. Once you change one or both nominalizations to verbs, you must then create subjects for those verbs.

FIRST ATTEMPT
The general is involved in a *discussion* of the *movement* of the troops.

Here we have the option to convert one or both of the nominalizations to their root verbs. To complete the sentence, we selected *general* as the new subject.

BETTER
The general *discussed* the movement of the troops.

or

The general *discussed* where the troops had *moved*.

FIRST ATTEMPT
The *withdrawal* of the troops was under *consideration* by the president.

In this situation, we can fix the original sentence by using *president* as the subject and converting one or both nominalizations to their root verbs.

BETTER
The president *considered* the withdrawal of the troops.

or

The president *considered* whether to *withdraw* the troops.

BRAIN TICKLERS
Set # 24

The following sentences suffer from nominal-ization overuse. Identify which of the four situations each sentence represents.

1. The admiration of the teacher by the class was apparent.

2. Our consideration of the matter is that it is unimportant.

3. Recognition and acceptance of a problem is the first step toward solving it.

4. Our solution to the problem is important to us.

5. The boys have no remembrance of their misdeed.

6. There is recognition of the player's effort.

7. The coach has come to the conclusion that his efforts are in vain.

8. There has been no indication by the strikers that they are giving in.

(Answers are on page 119.)

APPLYING THE TECHNIQUE

Now that you are skilled at identifying nominalizations, it is time to apply the second part of the Painless Technique and transform them into forceful verbs or descriptive adjectives.

FIRST ATTEMPT

Reorganizing Congress

Our Congress should begin *reorganization*. Predictably, there is *opposition* to this idea by most of the members of Congress. Nevertheless, the *acceptance* of the voters is with my idea. My first *inclination* would be to favor a *reduction* in the size of both legislative bodies because adequate *representation* could be accomplished with fewer elected officials. The lawmakers have given us the *indication* that their position is in our best interests. On the contrary, it is a *reflection* of their selfish concerns. (81)

This 81-word paragraph contains many nominalizations. As expected, it is full of weak verbs and contains many prepositional phrases, making it wordy. Let us see how to improve this paragraph. We begin with the first sentence:

Our Congress should begin *reorganization*.

This sentence illustrates Situation No. 1: A nominalization (*reorganization*) following a weak verb (*begin*). To improve this sentence, change the nominalization to its root verb, which can replace the weak verb. Our new sentence reads:

Our Congress should *reorganize*.

Let's examine the next sentence:

Predictably, there is *opposition* to this idea by most of the members of Congress.

This sentence is Situation No. 2: Nominalization inserted after an expletive construction (*there is*). Improve this sentence by converting the nominalization, which is *opposition*, to its root verb, *oppose*, and then specifically stating a subject to link to this more forceful verb. For our subject, let's use *most members of Congress*. Therefore, our improved sentence reads:

Predictably, most members of Congress *oppose* this idea.

Sentence No. 3:

Nevertheless, the *acceptance* of the voters is with my idea.

This sentence is similar to Situation No. 3, where the nominalization (*acceptance*) is the subject of a weak verb (*is*).

To improve this sentence, change the nominalization to its root verb form, *accept*, and use it to show the action of the real performers of the action, *the voters*.

Nevertheless, the voters *accept* my idea.

Sentence No. 4:

My first *inclination* would be to favor a *reduction* in the size of both legislative bodies because adequate *representation* could be accomplished with fewer elected officials.

Again, this is Situation No. 4: Consecutive nominalizations. This situation requires changing one or both nominalizations and then finding a subject for each verb. Transforming both nominalizations, we write

> I would be *inclined* toward *reducing* the size of both legislative bodies because Congress could adequately *represent* us with fewer elected officials.

Sentence No. 5:

> The lawmakers have given us the *indication* that their position is in our best interests.

This sentence depicts Situation No. 1 because the nominalization, *indication*, trails the weak verb, *have given*. We can improve this sentence by first transforming the nominalization to its root verb, *indicate*, and then replacing the original weak verb, *have given*, with the root verb. We write our new sentence:

> The lawmakers *indicate* that their position is in our best interests.

The final sentence:

> On the contrary, it is a *reflection* of their selfish concerns.

This is another Situation No. 1 sentence. Again, the technique requires us to change the nominalization, *reflection*, to its root verb form, *reflect*.

> On the contrary, it *reflects* their selfish concerns.

We're finished! Let's read the nominalization-reduced paragraph:

BETTER

Reorganizing Congress

Our Congress should reorganize. Predictably, most members of Congress oppose this idea. Nevertheless, the voters accept my idea. I would be inclined toward reducing the size of both legislative bodies because Congress could adequately represent us with fewer elected officials. The lawmakers indicate that their position is in our best interests. On the contrary, it reflects their selfish concerns. (59)

Not only is the excerpt clearer, it is less wordy. The rewritten paragraph contains 59 words. Recall that the original nominalization-ridden excerpt contained 81 words. Using the chapter's technique, not only have we made the paragraph clearer and more active, we have reduced the wordiness by more than 25 percent!

Surf's up...

Everyone is avoiding nominalizations, even in cyberspace. Check out this site:

www.webwritingthatworks.com/DGuideCOG5b.htm

Now it is your turn to transform nominalization-plagued sentences into lively and concise sentences.

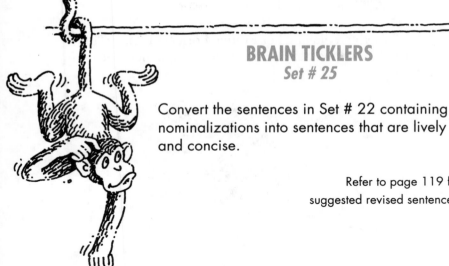

BRAIN TICKLERS
Set # 25

Convert the sentences in Set # 22 containing nominalizations into sentences that are lively and concise.

Refer to page 119 for suggested revised sentences.

NECESSARY NOMINALIZATION SITUATIONS

In some limited cases, nominalizations are useful, even necessary. Let's examine those limited situations that require nominalizations.

Situation no. 1: the nominalization is a subject referring to a previous sentence

John was late for school and lost his English notebook. His chronic *carelessness* brought about these predicaments.

Notice how the above nominalization, *carelessness*, helps link the second sentence to the first sentence.

> Katie practiced playing her French horn every day. This *dedication* helped her become an accomplished horn player.

Again, the nominalization, *dedication*, links the second sentence to the first.

Another instance in which nominalizations are necessary occurs where they represent concepts that are difficult to explain with only a few words.

Situation no. 2: nominalizations referring to well-known concepts

> The debate focused on the Flag Burning *Amendment*.

Rather than state that the debate focused on the revision or addition proposed to the Constitution of the United States, the writer simply uses the nominalization, *amendment*.

> *Freedom* of expression is certainly a charged topic open to debate.

Again, rather than write about the exemption from arbitrary restriction by civil authorities, the writer simply writes the nominalization, *freedom*.

As you can see, there are times when it is easier to describe familiar concepts rather than make your reader slog through a clause full of nouns and verbs. Concepts such as *death, love,* and *hate* are others that can be best expressed as nominalizations. Notice, however, that these will be infrequent situations, much like the passive voice exception of the last chapter. To follow this chapter's technique, perform this simple two-step process. First, determine whether the nominalization falls into one of the two exception situations. If not, then replace the nominalization with a forceful verb or a descriptive adjective.

BRAIN TICKLERS
Set # 26

The following paragraph is difficult to understand because it is filled with nominalizations. Transform the excerpt into a concise and interesting piece by reducing the nominalizations, where appropriate. After you have finished, take note of the reduced word count.

Writing Well

It is my contention that writing well is a matter of learning a few simple techniques. Ignorance of these techniques will no longer be a matter of acceptance by teachers. Therefore, there is no need for your acceptance of poor writing skills. Nonetheless, I know that your inclination is toward disagreement. However, I do not make this statement without the offer of proof. Take my suggestion, and try these techniques for one month. If after one month, you see no improvement, then seek other help. (85)

Refer to page 120 for a revised paragraph.

Practice makes permanent

Overusing nominalizations is detrimental, no matter what type of piece you are writing. As with all the other Painless Techniques, honing your new skill and making it a permanent part of your style should be your ultimate goal. Regularly, try the following to keep your technique sharp and part of your permanent writing style.

1. Using a previous writing assignment, examine it for nominalization overuse. Pull out a paragraph or two, and use your newly learned technique to make the excerpt more understandable and concise.

2. Select an excerpt from an exciting book you have read or are reading. First, notice the lack of nominalizations, and then rewrite a paragraph or two using some nominalizations and notice how they affect the clarity and flow of the writing.

Keep it flowing

This chapter's Painless Technique, as well as the previous chapters' Painless Techniques that you have mastered, will put you on the road to good writing. We can make it even more enjoyable by smoothing out the writing road. The next chapter shows how to make your writing flow across the pages.

BRAIN TICKLERS—THE ANSWERS

Set # 22, pages 100–101

1. The senator had no _recollection_ of his campaign promise. Attaching the suffix, -ion, to the root verb, _recollect_, forms the nominalization.

2. The teacher's _reaction_ to the news was a negative one. Attaching the suffix, -ion, to the root verb, _react_, forms the nominalization.

3. Each candidate is under *investigation* before his *nomination*.
   Attaching the suffix, *-ion*, to the root verb, *investigate*, forms the nominalization. Attaching the suffix, *-ion*, to the root verb, *nominate*, forms the second nominalization.

4. Many political prisoners have not had the benefit of *representation* by counsel.
   Attaching the suffix, *-ion*, to the root verb, *represent*, forms the nominalization.

5. The *discussion* of the class was on the field trip.
   Attaching the suffix, *-ion*, to the root verb, *discuss*, forms the nominalization.

6. The mayor's office started an *investigation* into the council member's actions.
   Attaching the suffix, *-ion*, to the root verb, *investigate*, forms the nominalization.

7. The husband and wife made a *renewal* of their wedding vows.
   Attaching the suffix, *-al*, to the root verb, *renew*, forms the nominalization.

8. The newspapers launched an *attack* of a vicious nature at the candidate.
   The writer uses the verb, *attack*, as a noun in this sentence.

9. The *induction* of the baseball player into the Hall of Fame took place on Friday.
   Attaching the suffix, *-ion*, to the root verb, *induct*, forms the nominalization.

10. Katie's *reaction* was predictable.
    Attaching the suffix, *-ion*, to the root verb, *react*, forms the nominalization.

11. Matthew made the *suggestion* that we stop at the campsite.
    Attaching the suffix, *-ion*, to the root verb, *suggest*, forms the nominalization.

12. The editorial is a *reflection* of the writer's thoughts.
Attaching the suffix, *-ion*, to the root verb, *reflect*, forms the nominalization.

13. Bob's writing *improvement* astounded everyone.
Attaching the suffix, *-ment*, to the root verb, *improve*, forms the nominalization.

14. The *carelessness* of his writing was apparent throughout the entire manuscript.
Attaching the suffix, *-ness*, to the root adjective, *careless*, forms the nominalization.

15. The general signaled for a *withdrawal* of his troops.
Attaching the suffix, *-al*, to the root verb, *withdraw*, forms the nominalization.

16. By your *acceptance* of this check, you agree to paint the house.
Attaching the suffix, *-ance*, to the root verb, *accept*, forms the nominalization.

Set # 23, page 103

The nominalizations are italicized.

The English Teacher

The English teacher had little *expectation* that her class would attain improvement in their writing. There are few *indications* that what she expects should be under *reconsideration*. However, a *discussion* among the students yielded a different *conclusion* because they were unwilling to make an *acceptance* of her conclusion. It was their *decision* to have a *discussion* with the principal about the *replacement* of their teacher. They realized, nevertheless, that the principal would have a *reluctance* to accept their *suggestion*.

Set # 24, pages 108–109

1. The admiration of the teacher by the class was apparent. (Situation No. 3: Nominalization is the subject of a weak verb)

2. Our consideration of the matter is that it is unimportant. (Situation No. 3: Nominalization is the subject of a weak verb)

3. Recognition and acceptance of a problem is the first step toward solving it. (Situation No. 4: Consecutive nominalizations)

4. Our solution to the problem is important to us. (Situation No. 3: Nominalization is the subject of a weak verb)

5. The boys have no remembrance of their misdeed. (Situation No. 1: Nominalization trails a weak verb)

6. There is recognition of the player's effort. (Situation No. 2: Nominalization following an expletive construction)

7. The coach has come to the conclusion that his efforts are in vain. (Situation No. 1: Nominalization trails a weak verb)

8. There has been no indication by the strikers that they are giving in. (Situation No. 2: Nominalization following an expletive construction)

Set # 25, page 113

1. The senator could not *recollect* his campaign promise.

2. The teacher *reacted* negatively to the news.

3. Before being *nominated*, each candidate is *investigated*.

4. Many political prisoners have not been represented by counsel.

5. The class *discussed* the field trip.

6. The mayor's office *investigated* the council member's actions.

7. The husband and wife *renewed* their wedding vows.

8. The newspapers viciously *attacked* the candidate.

9. The Hall of Fame *inducted* the baseball player on Friday.

10. Katie *reacted* predictably.

11. Matthew *suggested* that we stop at the campsite.

12. The editorial *reflected* the writer's thoughts.

13. Bob's *improved* writing astounded everyone.

14. The careless writing was apparent throughout the entire manuscript.

15. The general signaled his troops to *withdraw*.

16. By *accepting* this check, you agree to paint the house.

Set # 26, page 115

Writing Well

I contend that writing well is a matter of learning a few simple techniques. Teachers will no longer accept students ignoring these techniques. Therefore, there is no need for you to accept poor writing skills. Nonetheless, I know that you are inclined to disagree. However, I do not state this without offering proof. Do as I suggest, and try these techniques for one month. If after one month, you do not improve, then seek other help. (77)

CHAPTER FIVE

Smooth Out Your Writing

CONFRONTING CHOPPY WRITING

Has the word *choppy* ever been written on one of your papers? If so, your teacher was trying to tell you that your writing was stopping and starting with each new sentence, rather than smoothly flowing throughout. Choppy writing is a writing flaw that makes it difficult for your reader to follow what you have written. Poor transitions between sentences and between paragraphs are the main cause of choppy writing. Let's examine a choppy writing example entitled *Ms. Mahoney*.

Ms. Mahoney

Ms. Mahoney is an English teacher in my school. She is convinced that her students have been shortchanged. Ms. Mahoney spoke with the principal about developing a writing program. She had a program already worked out. The principal rejected her idea. The program had been set for the school year. She told her she would consider her request next year. Ms. Mahoney knows that will be too late for her students.

What makes *Ms. Mahoney* rather unpleasant to read? Read it again, but this time read it aloud. Notice how you stopped at the end of each sentence and how you had to begin again at the start of a new sentence. This paragraph is nothing more than a series of short, direct statements. Because this paragraph does not flow well, it is difficult for you to follow the writer's thoughts. Imagine reading page after page written in this stop-and-start style!

Let's take a look at the table below and see if it can help us. It sets forth the number of words and the sentence type in *Ms. Mahoney*.

Ms. Mahoney *Sentence Analysis*

Sentence	Number of Words	Type
1	9	Declarative
2	9	Declarative
3	11	Declarative
4	7	Declarative
5	5	Declarative
6	9	Declarative
7	10	Declarative
8	11	Declarative

The *Ms. Mahoney* paragraph typifies choppy writing. Consequently, we can assume that whatever makes this paragraph choppy probably causes a choppy style in other writing. Our sentence analysis table helps us locate the cause. Observe that every sentence is a declarative sentence containing 11 words or less. This means that you should watch for strings of short declarative sentences causing your reader to stop and start too frequently. Let's examine another sign of this poor writing style.

Read the following writing passage. Better yet, just as you did with *Ms. Mahoney*, read *Improving Writing Skills* aloud. Can you determine why it does not flow well?

Improving Writing Skills

It is my belief that the writing skills of any student can be improved. There is enough evidence in the form of compositions handed in before and after English courses. There are some students who benefit more than others from writing instruction. This is because they apply themselves.

It is a problem that can be easily corrected. There are programs that teachers, like myself, have created that can be immediately implemented. It is unfortunate, however, that there are teachers who are opposed to any methods that have not been previously used. It is of no consequence to them that "the way we have always done it" methods are ineffective.

Again, let's examine the passage one sentence at a time using a sentence structure table to help us spot any patterns.

Improving Writing Skills *Sentence Analysis*

Sentence	Words	Type	Introductory Words
1	14	Declarative	It is
2	16	Declarative	There is
3	12	Declarative	There are
4	6	Declarative	This is
5	9	Declarative	It is
6	14	Declarative	There are
7	20	Declarative	It is
8	18	Declarative	It is

Although the sentences are all declarative, they contain a significant number of words. Therefore, we don't seem to have the string of short declarative sentences problem. So what is the problem? Refer to the last column, *Introductory Words*. This column displays the words that begin each sentence. Notice the pattern?

The pattern is that every sentence begins with an **expletive construction**. We ran across expletive constructions in Chapter Four when we discussed the negative impact on your writing caused by overusing nominalizations. Well, they are back, and this time in the context of choppy writing. You will recall that a sentence beginning with the words *it* or *there* (*expletives*, in this instance) are followed by a form of the verb *be*, and the subject of the sentence is referred to as an *expletive construction*. Expletive constructions usually begin as follows:

There is . . .
It is . . .
There are . . .

Read through the passage *Improving Writing Skills* below. The expletives and their accompanying *be* verbs have been italicized. Notice how they prevent the sentences from flowing into one another, resulting in a piece of choppy writing.

Improving Writing Skills

It is my belief that the writing skills of any student can be improved. *There is* enough evidence in the form of compositions handed in before and after English courses. *There are* some students who benefit more than others from writing instruction. *This is* because they apply themselves.

It is a problem that can easily be corrected. *There are* programs that teachers, like myself, have created that can be immediately implemented. *It is* unfortunate, however, that there are teachers who are opposed to any methods that have not been previously used. *It is* of no consequence to them that "the way we have always done it" methods are ineffective.

Now, study a recent sample of your writing. If paragraph after paragraph contains several of these constructions, be aware that your sentences are weakly connected. By beginning nearly every sentence with an expletive construction, you set up your writing to be nothing more than a series of unconnected declarative sentences.

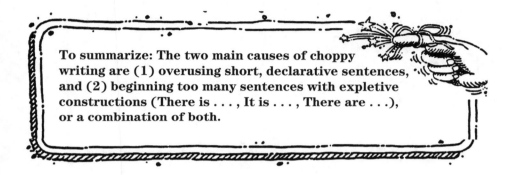

To summarize: The two main causes of choppy writing are (1) overusing short, declarative sentences, and (2) beginning too many sentences with expletive constructions (There is . . . , It is . . . , There are . . .), or a combination of both.

What you usually discover whenever you talk to students who have just written a choppy piece is that they feel their writing flows. Why? Because they smoothly linked the sentences in their mind, but not on their paper. That is why it is so important to spot the signs of choppy writing, because merely reading over your writing may not always help you catch your writing flaw.

This next exercise will help you make sure that you can spot the signs of choppy writing.

BRAIN TICKLERS
Set # 27

Good Writing Skills is an example of choppy writing. Identify the sentence structure that causes the stilted style.

Good Writing Skills

Good writing skills must be learned. Writing skills are like any other skill. It is well known that poor writers have improved their writing. There are many examples at both the middle school and high school level. There are some students who improve more than others. There is hope for everyone, however.

It is easy for students to improve their writing. I am one of those who improved. There are still times when I write poorly but they are not as numerous as before. It is a result of better writing that my grades have improved.

(Answers are on page 149.)

Now that you can spot the signs of choppy writing, you are ready to learn the Painless Technique for smoothing it out.

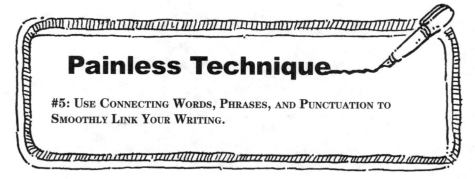

Painless Technique

#5: Use Connecting Words, Phrases, and Punctuation to Smoothly Link Your Writing.

SMOOTH YOUR WRITING BY LINKING YOUR SENTENCES

This chapter's technique employs three methods that will link your sentences together. By using these methods, you will avoid writing with only short declarative sentences and beginning too many of your sentences with expletive constructions.

Sentence linking method no. 1: Use linking words to connect sentences

The first method uses linking words. The concept underlying the first method is that each sentence should leave a "hook" for the sentence preceding it and the sentence following it. These hooks connect the consecutive sentences together in one of the following ways:

1. By *comparing* facts or concepts introduced in the consecutive sentences.

2. By making the consecutive sentences *reinforce* one another.

3. By making the consecutive sentences demonstrate a *consequence* of an action.

4. By allowing consecutive sentences to state information that follows in logical *continuity*.

When you use smooth transitions, your sentences will relate to one another by *comparison, reinforcement, consequence,* or *continuity*. Certain words, known as linking words, facilitate smooth transitions. The following table lists linking words by their functional category.

Comparison	Reinforcement	Consequence	Continuity
similarly	for instance	as a result	next
although	in addition	consequently	after
instead	for example	therefore	finally
nevertheless	moreover	thus	secondly
but	also	nevertheless	and

Examine the paragraph about Ms. Mahoney on page 123. Notice how the absence of linking words made it difficult to read. We can improve the paragraph's flow by combining the short declarative sentences to form complex ones, and then using linking words to hook the revised sentences. Let's see how we can improve *Ms. Mahoney*, beginning with the first two sentences:

> Ms. Mahoney is an English teacher in my school. She is convinced that her students have been shortchanged.

These two short declarative sentences can be combined into a longer sentence providing information connecting it to the next sentence.

> Ms. Mahoney, an English teacher in my school, is convinced that her students have been shortchanged in the development of their writing skills.

In the next sentence, we notice that it doesn't have a connecting hook to the previous sentence.

> Ms. Mahoney spoke with the principal about developing a writing program.

We can link this sentence to the first part of the paragraph by showing the *continuity* of Ms. Mahoney's actions.

> At the *beginning* of the school year, Ms. Mahoney spoke with the principal about developing a writing program for the students.

The next three sentences are weakly linked. Unfortunately, the writer probably envisioned their connection in his or her mind, but was unable to set it down on the paper.

> She had a program already worked out. The principal rejected her idea. The program had been set for the school year.

We can use *consequence* and *comparison* to hook the sentences to one another, as well as to the previous sentences.

> *Although* she had a program already worked out, the principal rejected her idea *because* the program had been set for the school year.

The next sentence is another short declarative sentence standing alone.

> She told her she would consider her request next year.

We can use *comparison* to link it to the previous sentence.

> *Instead*, she told her that maybe the school would consider her request next year.

The last sentence does little to complete the paragraph because it relates poorly to the preceding sentences.

> Ms. Mahoney knows that will be too late for her students.

We can use *consequence* to hook this sentence to the preceding sentences and provide a conclusion for the paragraph.

> *Nonetheless*, Ms. Mahoney knows that it will be too late for her students.

Now compare the revised passage to the original one, and notice how well the sentences flow and how much more enjoyable it is to read.

BETTER

Ms. Mahoney

Ms. Mahoney, an English teacher in my school, is convinced that her students have been shortchanged in the development of their writing skills. At the beginning of the school year, Ms. Mahoney spoke with the principal about developing a writing program for the students. Although she had a program already worked out, the principal rejected her idea because the program had been set for the school year. Instead, she told her that maybe the school would consider her request next year. Nonetheless, Ms. Mahoney knows that it will be too late for her students.

Surf's up...

The next time you are surfing, check out the following site that discusses transitions between sentences:

https://writing.wise/edu/Handbook/Transitions/html

You have seen how linking words that create hooks between sentences improve the flow of a writing piece. Now it is your turn to try using linking words to create smooth transitions between sentences.

BRAIN TICKLERS
Set # 28

Rewrite the following paragraph using the first method of this chapter's Painless Technique for smoothing out choppy writing. Your goal should be to create hooks that smoothly link the sentences.

Summertime

Our family enjoys summer vacation. We usually go on a long trip. My aunt lives in New Orleans. We often travel to see her. Sometimes she comes to our house. We go on a trip together. We went to the Grand Canyon last year. We really enjoyed ourselves.

See page 149 for a possible revision.

In your revised paragraph, notice how you enabled the shorter sentences to work together. This made it easier for the reader to envision the sequence of events. Let's examine another of the Painless Technique's methods for smoothing choppy writing.

Sentence linking method no. 2: Use demonstrative pronouns and relative pronouns to link sentences

A *demonstrative pronoun* is a pronoun that refers to a specific person, place, or thing. Examples of demonstrative pronouns are

- *This*
- *That*
- *These*
- *Those*

We can use the reference created by the demonstrative pronoun to connect sentences. Let's see how to do this with the following piece of choppy writing.

FIRST ATTEMPT

Away from Home

John could not wait to leave home and go off to college. He told his parents every day. He looked at going away to college as going on a vacation. He would come to find out he was incredibly wrong. He spent every night in the library studying until midnight. He recalled what he had said to his parents.

The paragraph set out statements in a boring stop-and-start style. The second linking method can help us. Let's look at the first two sentences:

John could not wait to leave home and go off to college. He told his parents every day.

The writer has related the two short declarative sentences, but not connected them. We can link the two sentences with a demonstrative pronoun.

> John could not wait to leave home and go off to college,
> and he told his parents *this* every day.

The demonstrative pronoun, *this*, connects the second sentence to the first sentence. Let's tackle the next two sentences:

> He looked at going away to college as going on
> a vacation. He would come to find out he was
> incredibly wrong.

Again, these two relatively short declarative sentences do not connect. Again, we can turn to demonstrative pronouns for help.

> He looked at going away to college as going on a
> vacation. *That* idea, he would come to find out, was
> incredibly wrong.

Notice how we can relate the second sentence back to the first one by beginning the second sentence with *that idea.* Proceeding to the next two sentences:

> He spent every night in the library studying until
> midnight. He recalled what he had said to his parents.

Here again we are confronted by short declarative sentences that do not connect and do not do a good job of wrapping up the paragraph. We can remedy that shortcoming with a demonstrative pronoun.

> Every night *that* he was in the library studying until
> midnight, he recalled *those* words he had said to his
> parents.

Now, as you compare the rewritten passage to the original one, notice how the demonstrative pronouns helped the paragraph flow from one sentence to the next.

Away from Home

John could not wait to leave home and go off to college, and he told his parents this every day. He looked at going away to college as going on a vacation. That idea, he would come to find out, was incredibly wrong. Every night that he was in the library studying until midnight, he recalled those words he had said to his parents.

Demonstrative pronouns provide you with another way to combat choppy writing, and with a little practice, you will have no trouble using this method. Let's give it a try!

BRAIN TICKLERS
Set # 29

Use demonstrative pronouns to link the sentences in *The Mascot.*

The Mascot

Our high school does not have a mascot. Many of the students were upset because the school was without a mascot. The students decided to run a contest to see who could select the best mascot. The contest turned into a disaster. The students wanted a cute mascot. A cute mascot would show how friendly our school was. A cute mascot was unacceptable to the basketball players. The basketball players wanted the mascot to be ferocious looking. The principal had to end the contest. We still do not have a mascot.

Refer to page 149 for a possible revision.

USING RELATIVE PRONOUNS

You have seen how demonstrative pronouns linked several disconnected sentences; relative pronouns can perform the same service. Recall that a *relative pronoun* refers to a person, place, or thing that preceded it. Examples of relative pronouns are

- *Who*
- *Which*
- *Where*
- *That*

This referencing function serves to link the present and preceding sentence. Let's see how this works. First, read the version of *Country Living* without the relative pronoun connectors.

FIRST ATTEMPT

Country Living

I love the serenity of the country. It is the place that recharges me. I can be myself there. My closest neighbors are the Bradfords. They live over a mile away. They are wonderful people. I cannot think of anywhere else that I could live so well.

Next, read the same paragraph, but now the writer has taken advantage of relative pronouns. Notice how relative pronouns link the ideas and facts of the preceding sentence to its following sentence in this excerpt.

BETTER

Country Living

I love the serenity of the country. It is the place that recharges me, and one *where* I can be myself. My closest neighbors, the Bradfords, *who* live over a mile away, are wonderful people. *Where* else could one live so well?

Now it is your turn to use relative pronouns to improve a piece of choppy writing.

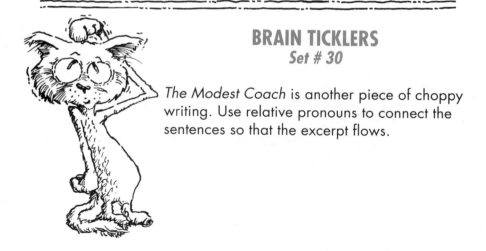

BRAIN TICKLERS
Set # 30

The Modest Coach is another piece of choppy writing. Use relative pronouns to connect the sentences so that the excerpt flows.

The Modest Coach

I was surprised when the team won all of its games. I do not know if anyone was expecting the team to win every game. Warren Peese gave the credit to the players. He has been the coach of the school for 15 years and has always avoided praising himself. Most coaches would not have missed the opportunity to take at least some credit.

Refer to page 150 for a possible revision.

USING SEMICOLONS

You have seen how the second sentence linking method uses relative and demonstrative pronouns to create smooth transitions between sentences. Now let's investigate the last of this technique's methods to make your writing flow smoothly. This method involves linking certain sentences with a semicolon.

Sentence linking method no. 3: Use a semicolon to link closely related statements

Many writers avoid using semicolons because they are not sure when they are appropriate. The next chapter discusses their use in more detail, but for now, it is enough to say that a semicolon links two closely related facts or concepts.

FIRST ATTEMPT
Maria quit her job. She thought about it a lot. She knew she made the right decision.

BETTER
Maria quit her job; she thought about it a lot and knew she made the right decision.

Notice how the semicolon links Maria's actions in the first short declarative sentence with her thought process revealed by the two short declarative sentences that followed. Let's review another example where the semicolon helps connect short-declarative sentences.

FIRST ATTEMPT

Matt is the best speaker in the school. He is the leader on the speech and debate team.

Again, we are confronted with short declarative sentences. Therefore, we can use a semicolon to combine the short sentences into one flowing sentence.

BETTER

Matt is the best speaker in the school; he is the leader on the speech and debate team.

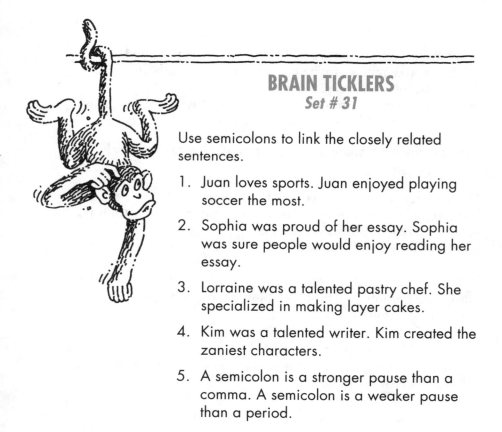

BRAIN TICKLERS
Set # 31

Use semicolons to link the closely related sentences.

1. Juan loves sports. Juan enjoyed playing soccer the most.

2. Sophia was proud of her essay. Sophia was sure people would enjoy reading her essay.

3. Lorraine was a talented pastry chef. She specialized in making layer cakes.

4. Kim was a talented writer. Kim created the zaniest characters.

5. A semicolon is a stronger pause than a comma. A semicolon is a weaker pause than a period.

Refer to page 150 for some possible sentences.

You have now mastered the three sentence linking methods. Keep them in mind whenever you are writing. You can refer to the summary below:

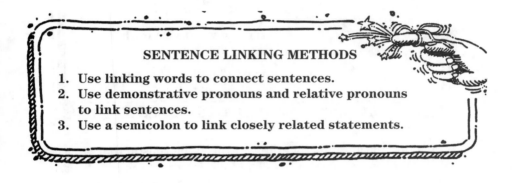

SENTENCE LINKING METHODS

1. **Use linking words to connect sentences.**
2. **Use demonstrative pronouns and relative pronouns to link sentences.**
3. **Use a semicolon to link closely related statements.**

DEBATE TEAM

TRANSITIONING PARAGRAPHS

We have seen how it is important to connect sentences within the paragraph, but it is also important to connect the paragraphs within the entire essay. Disconnected paragraphs lead to the same choppy writing caused by disconnected sentences. Just as it lacks smoothly flowing sentence-to-sentence transitions, many students' writing lacks smooth transitions between paragraphs. Let's examine how we can correct that writing flaw.

Surf's up...

Here is a great site for help with linking paragraphs:

http://writingcenter.unc.edu/handouts/transitions

We link paragraphs together for the same reason that we link sentences to one another. The following three methods can be employed to connect your paragraphs, and thereby create a smooth flow to your writing submission.

Paragraph linking method no. 1: Use introductory linking words and phrases

The first method suggests opening each paragraph with a linking word or phrase. Let's see how this works by first looking at an excerpt where the writer failed to link the paragraphs.

FIRST ATTEMPT

One expert on military affairs determined that we are in a more perilous situation now with the collapse of the Soviet Union than we have ever been. He argues that the so-called "peace dividend" is wishful thinking by Americans. Terrorism and growing third world military powers have replaced the controlled might of the Soviet Union.

The United States must be more on its guard, not only outside of its borders, but inside as well. Expenditures for military and security forces will increase rather than decrease, as many politicians are fond of telling their constituents. This means even less available money for social problems than during the Cold War days.

Americans are truly much safer from the threat of a world war than they have been in the last 100 years, and that is good news for all of us.

Notice how the writing sample below connects the paragraphs with a linking word or a linking phrase.

BETTER

> One expert on military affairs determined that we are in a more perilous situation now with the collapse of the Soviet Union than we have ever been. He argues that the so-called "peace dividend" is wishful thinking by Americans. Terrorism and growing third world military powers have replaced the controlled might of the Soviet Union.
>
> *Thus*, the United States will have to be more on its guard, not only outside of its borders, but inside as well. Expenditures for military and security forces will increase rather than decrease, as many politicians are fond of telling their constituents. This means even less available money for social problems than during the Cold War days.
>
> *Nevertheless*, in spite of this gloomy news, Americans are truly much safer from the threat of a world war than they have been in the last 100 years, and that is good news for all of us.

Paragraph linking method no. 2: Use repeating key words

The second method for linking paragraphs involves using a key word at the end of one paragraph, and then repeating it at the beginning of the next paragraph. Notice below how the key word *interest* links the facts of the first paragraph to the hoped-for consequence in the second paragraph. First, however, let's look at the disconnected excerpt.

FIRST ATTEMPT

> The candidates engaged one another in a series of debates throughout the state. The debates were lightly attended, but were viewed by many voters on television. The candidates were surprised by the voters' interest. Apathy toward statewide elections was common in the past.
>
> The candidates are hoping for a 50 percent voter turnout, rather than the usual 20 percent.

BETTER

> The candidates engaged one another in a series of debates throughout the state. The debates were lightly attended, but were viewed by many voters on television. The candidates were surprised by the voters' *interest*. Apathy toward statewide elections was common in the past.
>
> The candidates are hoping this *interest* in the debates carries over into the voting booths on election day. They are hoping for a 50 percent voter turnout, rather than the usual 20 percent.

Paragraph linking method no. 3: Ask and then answer a question

The last method involves finishing one paragraph with a question, then answering the question in the following paragraph. Notice in the revised excerpt how the second paragraph links the first and third paragraph by answering the first paragraph's question and posing a question for the third paragraph to address.

First, the disconnected excerpt:

FIRST ATTEMPT

Teachers from all over the United States are attending the national conference. The conference is noted for encouraging dialogue concerning difficult issues facing the teachers. The conference agenda is packed with discussion items. One receiving the most attention deals with programs and techniques for helping students to write better.

Writing is a skill activity, and like all skill activities, repetition is the key to success. We encourage athletes and musicians to practice and hone their skills. We should do the same with student writing.

Many argue that writing differs from sports and music because athletes and musicians require only muscle repetition to attain proficiency, whereas writing proficiency requires applying certain techniques to abstract thoughts.

BETTER

Teachers from all over the United States are attending the national conference. The conference is noted for encouraging dialogue concerning difficult issues facing the teachers. The conference agenda is packed with discussion items, but the one receiving the most attention deals with the question: *"How can we help our students write better?"*

In spite of the complexity of the question, *the answer may be as simple as, "Just make them write more."* Writing is a skill activity, and like all skill activities, repetition is the key to success. We encourage athletes and musicians to practice and hone their skills; *why not take the same road with student writing?*

Educators respond to this suggestion differently. Many argue that writing differs from sports and music because athletes and musicians require only muscle repetition to attain proficiency, whereas writing proficiency requires applying certain techniques to abstract thoughts.

When confronted with composing a piece with several pages of paragraphs, the above three methods should be used in variety so as not to make the piece sound trite by using predictable paragraph transitions. To recap, listed below are this chapter's methods for linking sentences and paragraphs. If you use these, you will never have the word *choppy* written on your paper again.

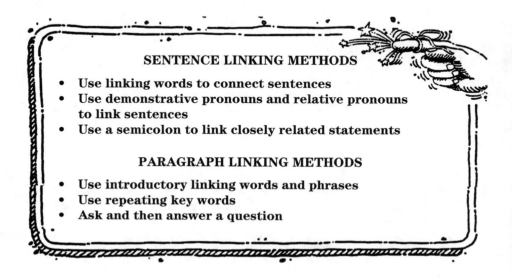

SENTENCE LINKING METHODS

- Use linking words to connect sentences
- Use demonstrative pronouns and relative pronouns to link sentences
- Use a semicolon to link closely related statements

PARAGRAPH LINKING METHODS

- Use introductory linking words and phrases
- Use repeating key words
- Ask and then answer a question

Now you should be ready to use all of this chapter's Painless Technique methods to smooth out your writing.

BRAIN TICKLERS
Set # 32

Use the Painless Technique's methods to link the sentences within the paragraphs, as well as for linking the paragraphs of *Stress in Our Contemporary World.*

Stress in Our Contemporary World

Eating and exercise habits affect a person's health. Heredity plays a part in determining a person's longevity too. Some scientists believe stress affects a person's health. They are trying to determine why people are under more stress today than they were a generation ago. They are also trying to find a way to alleviate that stress. I feel that stress grows as civilization progresses. Other researchers do not embrace my view.

There are more people in the world today than there ever have been. This is one cause for the increasing level of stress. Information moves faster than it ever has. There is also more of it. Civilization cannot progress without people and information.

The interaction of people and information will be important in the future. Studies show that we can be overloaded with information. This makes people anxious, and even violent. We should seek solutions to these problems.

Refer to page 150 for one possible revision.

Practice makes permanent

You should realize that choppy writing is a serious writing flaw. By learning these Painless Technique's methods for smoothing out your writing, you are well on your way to dramatically improving your writing style. As always, honing your new skill and making it a permanent part of your style should be your ultimate goal. Try the following, perhaps once a week, to keep this technique sharp.

1. Examine a previous writing assignment for choppy writing. Pull out a paragraph or two, and use the Painless Technique's methods to help the writing flow.

2. Select three or four nonconsecutive paragraphs from a magazine article. Using linking words, phrases, and sentences, try to create a smooth transition between the paragraphs. This is a hard one, but give it a try!

KEEP YOUR WRITING FLOWING

With a little practice, your writing should flow across the pages. This chapter's techniques and the techniques that you have learned in other chapters will greatly improve your writing style—but we are not yet through. Many bad writing habits, such as passive voice writing and using too many short declarative statements, are often rooted in a writer's inability to punctuate the longer compound and complex sentences. Why is this?

One answer is that students who are uncomfortable with their ability to punctuate these sentences will often write short, choppy sentences. The problem emanates from their lack of skill using the simple comma to punctuate the more complex sentences. If you are one of these students, the next chapter demonstrates a technique that shows you how to use the comma to transform short, choppy sentences into longer, flowing ones.

BRAIN TICKLERS—THE ANSWERS

Set # 27, page 128

Good Writing Skills

Good writing skills must be learned. (Short declarative sentence) Writing skills are like any other skill. (Short declarative sentence) It is (expletive construction) well known that poor writers have improved their writing. There are (expletive construction) many examples at both the middle school and high school levels. There are (expletive construction) some students who improve more than others. There is (expletive construction) hope for everyone, however.

   It is (expletive construction) easy for students to improve their writing. I am one of those who improved. (short declarative sentence) There are (expletive construction) still times when I write poorly but they are (expletive construction) not as numerous as before. It is (expletive construction) as a result of better writing that my grades have improved.

Set # 28, page 133

Summertime

Our family enjoys summer vacation. Consequently, we usually go on a long trip. (Consequence) My aunt lives in New Orleans, *and* we often travel to see her (Continuity), *although* sometimes she comes to our house *so that* we can go on a trip together. (Comparison and consequence) *For instance*, we went to the Grand Canyon last year, *and* we really enjoyed ourselves. (Reinforcement and continuity)

Set # 29, pages 136–137

The Mascot

Our high school does not have a mascot, and *this* upset many of the students. *They* decided to run a contest to see who could select the best mascot. *This* turned into a disaster. Some students wanted a cute mascot *that* would show how friendly our school was. *This* was unacceptable to the basketball players. *These* players wanted the mascot to be ferocious looking. The principal had to end the contest, and *that* is why we still do not have a mascot.

Set # 30, pages 138–139

The Modest Coach

I was surprised when the team won all of its games. *Who* would have expected them to win every game? Warren Pease, *who* has been the coach of the school for 15 years, gave the credit to the players. He has always avoided praising himself. *Where* else can you find a coach *who* would not take at least some credit?

Set # 31, page 140

1. Juan loves sports; he enjoyed playing soccer the most.
2. Sophia was proud of her essay; she was sure people would enjoy reading it.
3. Lorraine was a talented pastry chef; her specialty was layer cakes.
4. Kim was a talented writer; she created the zaniest characters.
5. A semicolon is a stronger pause than a comma; however, it is a weaker pause than a period.

Set # 32, page 147

Stress in Our Contemporary World

Eating and exercise habits affect a person's health. *However,* heredity plays a part in determining a person's longevity too. Some scientists believe stress affects a person's health, and *consequently,* they are trying to determine why people are under more stress today than they were a generation ago. *Furthermore,* they are also trying to find a way to alleviate that stress. I feel that stress grows as civilization progresses, *although* other researchers *do not embrace my view.*

Yet, they cannot disagree that there are more people in the world today than there ever have been. This is one cause for the increasing level of stress. *For instance,* information moves faster than it ever has, *and* there is also more of it. *Why is this important to our progress?*

How people and information interact will be important to our future because this will determine the quality of our progress. For example, studies show that we can be overloaded with information, and this makes people anxious, and even violent. *Therefore,* we should seek solutions to these problems.

CHAPTER SIX

Harness the Power of the Comma

POLISHING YOUR WRITING WITH COMMAS

Do short sentences dominate your writing? You may recall one of your English teachers telling you that a simple sentence consists of a single *independent clause* and no *dependent clauses*. Unfortunately, that definition does not tell us much unless we first understand what a clause is, and then understand independent and dependent clauses. So, let's take a look at them.

A *clause* is a group of words that includes a subject *and* a verb. A clause can be distinguished from a *phrase*, which is a group of words that has *either* a subject or a verb, but not both. There are two kinds of clauses—independent clauses and dependent clauses. An independent clause is a clause that can stand alone as a sentence, which means it has a subject and a verb and expresses a complete thought. By comparison, a dependent clause is a clause containing a subject and a verb; however, it does not express a complete thought. Therefore, a dependent clause cannot constitute a complete sentence and must be paired with one or more independent clauses to create a sentence. Within the sentence, a dependent clause is introduced either by subordinate conjunctions or relative pronouns.

The table below sets out the common **subordinate conjunctions** and **relative pronouns**.

Subordinate Conjunctions	Relative Pronouns
unless	which
if	who
after	that
once	whom
rather	whose
because	

The <u>dependent clauses</u> are italicized in the sentences below.

> *Because the students had done so well on the test,* the teacher gave them the day off.
>
> *If you enjoy writing,* you should enroll in Dr. Novo's English class.
>
> Our band, *which meets every Wednesday after school,* will perform in the school auditorium next week.
>
> Jenny, *who is our class president,* is always trying to make her friends aware of important social issues.

In contrast, an <u>independent clause</u> is a clause containing a subject and a predicate that can stand alone as a complete sentence.

> Because the students had done so well on the test, *the teacher gave them the day off.*
>
> If you enjoy writing, *you should take Dr. Novo's English class.*
>
> *Our band,* which meets every Wednesday after school, *will perform in the school auditorium next week.*
>
> *Jenny,* who was our class president, *was always trying to make her friends aware of important social issues.*

As you see, an independent clause is a simple sentence, and because simple sentences consist of only one independent clause, most simple sentences are brief. Below are some examples of typical simple sentences.

> The teacher entered the classroom.
> The car ran off the road.
> The student finished the writing assignment.

As we learned in the previous chapter, writing with only short, simple sentences, such as those in the example, may create a choppy piece of writing. However, this chapter's Painless Technique will help you to avoid that writing flaw.

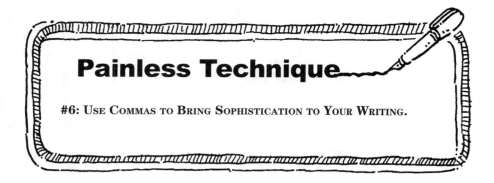

Painless Technique

#6: Use Commas to Bring Sophistication to Your Writing.

You will see how the comma helps create long, flowing sentences because it enables you to address several concepts in one sentence. In this chapter we discuss a few simple methods for using the comma to make your writing flow and better present your ideas.

GROWING BEYOND
THE SIMPLE SENTENCE

An effective way to improve your writing is to progress from a simple style to a sophisticated style. You can do that by replacing short, simple sentences expressing only a single concept with long, flowing sentences that address multiple concepts. Consequently, we want to move beyond that plain style with its simple sentences, and we can do that, in part, just by using the simple but powerful *comma*.

These sophisticated sentences that we are striving to write to break up the monotony of choppy sentences fall into three categories.

Compound sentences

The first category of sentences capable of expressing multiple concepts is the *compound sentence*. A compound sentence contains two or more independent clauses, but no dependent clauses. Notice in the following examples of compound sentences how a comma and a coordinating conjunction join the independent clauses. A coordinating conjunction is a conjunction that joins pairs of a sentence that are grammatically equal, such as two or more independent clauses. The coordinating conjunctions are: *and, but, or, nor, for, yet,* and *so.*

> I went to John's house, but he was not home.
> The student studied all night, yet he failed the test.
> The band performed on Tuesday, but their Wednesday
>   performance was canceled.

Compound sentences constitute the first step toward moving beyond simple sentences. By moving from the simple to compound sentence, we can compare or link events and ideas that were confined to separate sentences. Moreover, because compound sentences are usually longer sentences, we can use them to help make the passage read smoothly. Now, let's look at the next category of sophisticated sentences, the complex sentence.

Complex sentences

A *complex sentence* is a sentence that includes one independent clause and one or more dependent clauses. Notice how the comma separates the dependent clause (single underline) from the independent clause (double underline) in the following complex sentences.

> Because clear-cut forests hold less water, the vegetation
>   suffers.
> After leaving Pittsburgh, Katie moved to California.
> If you enjoy writing, you should try to read books
>   suggested by your teacher.

Complex sentences provide us with an even greater framework within which to express multiple concepts, and like compound sentences, including them in your writing makes the passage flow smoothly. Now we move on to the most sophisticated of the sentences, the compound-complex sentence.

Compound-complex sentences

The *compound-complex sentence* is constructed by using two or more independent clauses and at least one dependent clause. Notice how the powerful comma separates the dependent clause (single underline) from the independent clauses (double underline).

While Matt was sleeping, his parents decorated the house for his birthday and his sister baked him a cake.
At the mayor's request, the city council adjourned and the city controller resigned.

Surf's up...

If you want to know more about these sophisticated sentences, the following web site is for you:

http://www.english-grammar.revolution.com/compound-complex-sentence.html

BRAIN TICKLERS
Set # 33

Read each sentence below and identify whether it is a simple, compound, complex, or compound-complex sentence.

1. I know my writing is choppy, and I need to improve it.

2. Although my writing is choppy, I'm not sure how to improve it.

3. My writing is choppy.

4. During the summer, I discovered my writing was choppy, and I learned how to write flowing sentences.

(Answers are on page 176.)

THREE METHODS FOR CREATING SOPHISTICATED SENTENCES

Our goal is to use commas to combine two or more simple sentences into a flowing compound, complex, or compound-complex sentence. With that goal in mind, this chapter's Painless Technique provides three methods for using the powerful comma to improve your writing.

Method no. 1: Use a comma with an introductory phrase

A stubby declarative sentence often can be transformed to an introductory phrase, then combined with another short sentence or sentences to form a flowing sentence. Let us examine the two categories of phrases that work particularly well as introductory phrases. Let's begin with the participial phrase and the preepositional phrase.

The Participial Phrase

A *participial phrase* begins with a participle, which is merely the verb form of a word that ends with *-ing* (present participle) or *-ed* (past participle). The phrase includes additional words that, together with the participle, function as an adjective.

PRESENT PARTICIPIAL PHRASES

Disappearing into the crowd, the thief eluded the police.

Scavenging for an easy meal, the gulls help to keep the beach clean.

PAST PARTICIPIAL PHRASES

Scared to ring the doorbell, the children stood frozen at the door.

Elated with her test scores, Jennifer applied to Harvard and Stanford.

The following examples demonstrate the method of converting a declarative sentence to a participial phrase, and then combining the phrase with another sentence to create a more sophisticated sentence.

FIRST ATTEMPT

John was bored with life. He set out to see the world. The first leg of his trip was going to take him to Mexico City. (26)

Let's work on those first two short sentences. By rewriting the first sentence into a participial phrase, *bored with life*, and using it as an introductory phrase for the subsequent sentence, we can transform the passage.

BETTER

Bored with life, John set out to travel the world. The first leg of his trip was going to take him to Mexico City. (24)

This method cuts down on wordiness by eliminating common words in both of the short sentences. For instance, in the above example, we eliminated the pronoun reference to the subject, *John*, in the second sentence (*he*), as well as the weak verb, *was*, in the first sentence.

Below is another example illustrating a situation in which we can convert a short declarative sentence into a participial phrase and then use it as an introductory phrase for a more sophisticated sentence.

FIRST ATTEMPT

Marty has studied grammar. Therefore, she felt more comfortable in her writing. (12)

Transform the above sentences by changing the first sentence into the participial phrase *having studied grammar*. Then use it as an introductory phrase to create a complex sentence.

BETTER

Having studied grammar, Marty felt more comfortable in her writing. (10)

Again, notice the decreased number of words in the revised sentence. Not only does the passage flow better, but it is less wordy. Let's look at one last example of converting a simple sentence into a participial phrase and then using this phrase to introduce the second sentence.

FIRST ATTEMPT
Margaret was excited by her progress. She moved on to the next lesson. (13)

Converting the first sentence into a participial phrase, *excited by her progress*, and then using it to introduce the subsequent sentence can improve the above passage. Notice the word count of both passages.

BETTER
Excited by her progress, Margaret moved on to the next lesson. (11)

Surf's up...

The following web site provides examples of the power of the comma in improving your writing:

http://www.thepunctuationguide.com/comma.html

Watch out!

Beware of the dangling participle! A *dangling participle* is a participle that is not correctly related to the noun it is supposed to modify. Notice that in all of the above examples, the participial phrase refers to the subject of the sentence. Let's take a look at some additional examples.

Having studied grammar, Marty felt more comfortable in her writing.

The participial phrase, *having studied grammar*, refers to the subject of the sentence, *Marty*. The sentence makes sense when this relationship between the participial phrase and the subject remains intact. Let's look for this relationship in another example.

Excited by her progress, Margaret moved on to the next lesson.

Likewise, the participial phrase, *excited by her progress*, refers to the subject of the sentence, *Margaret*. The sentence makes it clear that Margaret is progressing because she is encouraged by her progress. By contrast, let's examine what happens when the writer uses a dangling particple and incorrectly modifies the wrong noun in the sentence with a participial phrase.

Having recently died, I thought of Jim every day.

How can you think of someone when you are dead? Obviously, the writer meant that the subject, *I*, thought of the recently deceased, *Jim*, every day. Unfortunately, the writer modified *I* rather than *Jim* with the participial phrase. Watch out for those dangling participles! To avoid them, carefully read what you have written to ensure that you haven't accidentally used a dangling participle.

The above examples showed you how a participial phrase can make your writing flow. Now try the following exercise to see if you can use participial phrases to convert short simple sentences to a flowing sentence.

BRAIN TICKLERS
Set # 34

For each pair of sentences, change one sentence to a participial phrase so that it acts as an introductory phrase for the second sentence. When you are finished, the two simple sentences should be combined into one flowing sentence. Also, take note of the word count in your revised sentence.

1. Joe was angered by Tim. He slammed down the telephone. (10)

2. Mary is very embarrassed to participate in class. She answered a question for the first time yesterday. (17)

3. The students were interested in learning about toads. They listened closely to their teacher. (14).

4. Jason was excited at the thought of receiving presents. He stayed up all night. He was the first one in the living room on Christmas Day. (26)

5. When we leave depends upon the weather. We will leave tomorrow if the weather is close to being pleasant. (19)

6. The baby is sitting in his high chair. He is waiting to be fed. (14)

7. The hermit was removed from society. He had little use for contemporary technological advances. (14)

8.   The young jockey had just won the Kentucky Derby. She now set her sights on the prestigious Preakness. (18)

(Answers are on page 176.)

You have seen how the participial phrase and the comma can help make your writing flow. Now look at the other type of phrase, the prepositional phrase, that, together with the comma, can improve your writing.

The Prepositional Phrase

We have already learned about *prepositional phrases*, which are phrases that begin with a preposition and include the preposition's object (underlined) and its modifiers. Below are some examples of prepositional phrases.

With the flow
Under the oak tree
Against all odds

Another way to create an introductory phrase is to convert a simple sentence to a prepositional phrase and then set the phrase off with a comma so that it forms an introductory clause for a complex or compound-complex sentence. Let's look at an example with two simple sentences.

FIRST ATTEMPT
The eighth-graders performed the opening act. The characters were angry at each other.

Converting the first sentence into a prepositional phrase, *in the opening act performed by the eighth-graders*, and then using it as an introductory phrase for the subsequent sentence can transform the above sentence into a complex sentence.

BETTER
In the opening act performed by the eighth-graders, the characters were angry at each other.

Again, we see how two simple sentences can be transformed into a flowing complex sentence by creating a prepositional phrase set off by a comma.

FIRST ATTEMPT

The moon glowed overhead. The boys enjoyed the stillness of the night.

Converting the first sentence into a prepositional phrase, *with the moon glowing overhead*, and then using a comma to set it off from the second sentence, we can write a flowing complex sentence that expresses moroe than a single concept.

BETTER

With the moon glowing overhead, the boys enjoyed the stillness of the night.

Prepositional phrases play the same important role as participial phrases. Together, these two types of phrases, in conjunction with the comma, help to make your writing flow and comprise the first method of this chapter's Painless Technique. Before we move on to the next two methods associated with our Painless Technique, work through the following exercise to make sure you can use prepositional phrases.

BRAIN TICKLERS
Set # 35

For each pair of sentences below, convert one sentence to a prepositional phrase that can be used as an introductory phrase for a complex sentence.

1. The team played their hearts out in the first game. They continued to play that way throughout the season.

2. I won first place in the writing competition. I worked hard.

3. Buying the boat was against his better judgment. He bought the sailboat.

4. The antagonist and protagonist opened the play. They were engaged in a very long dialogue scene.

5. His parents waved good-bye to their son. He raced off to enjoy his newfound freedom as a college student.

6. Mr. Jones voted for the current mayor. He might have voted for the challenger if the circumstances were different.

7. Sarah's English teacher accompanied her. They left for the meeting with the principal at two o'clock.

(Answers are on pages 176–177.)

Together, the introductory phrase and the comma are powerful tools that you can use to smooth out choppy writing. Let's examine another method that utilizes the comma to improve writing plagued by numerous simple sentences.

Method no. 2: Use a comma and a coordinating conjunction to link simple sentences

The second method of this chapter's Painless Technique uses the comma and a coordinating conjunction to join two independent clauses (simple sentences) to create a flowing sentence. Recall that an *independent clause* is a group of words containing a subject and verb, and expresses a complete thought. Commas can link independent clauses only if they have the help of a coordinating conjunction. Recall from earlier in the chapter that the usual coordinating conjunctions are *and, but, or, nor, so, for,* and *yet.* Let's see how this method works by looking at the following examples where two independent clauses create a choppy writing segment.

FIRST ATTEMPT

The students respect Ms. Martin. Similarly, she respects her class.

The choppy clauses form a longer, smoother sentence after being linked with a comma and the coordinating conjunction, *and.* Now we have:

BETTER

The students respect Ms. Martin, *and* she respects her class.

Let's try the method again on the following bit of choppy writing.

FIRST ATTEMPT

Ms. Martin wanted to be a writer. Her fondness for children convinced her to teach.

Here, the independent clauses or simple sentences can form a longer sentence by connecting them with a comma and the coordinating conjunction, *but.*

BETTER

Ms. Martin wanted to be a writer, *but* her fondness for children convinced her to teach.

It is important to remember that this method requires *both* the comma and the coordinating conjunction to join two or more independent clauses, and that omitting the coordinating conjunction creates a writing error known as the *comma splice*. The following example illustrates this common writing error.

FIRST ATTEMPT

The composition is terribly choppy, only a complete rewrite will help it.

This is a typical attempt by a writer to combine two short sentences into a longer sentence by using a comma; however, a comma splice results, thus making the sentence grammatically incorrect and difficult to understand. To correct this writing error, a coordinating conjunction such as *and* is needed.

BETTER

The composition is terribly choppy, *and* only a complete rewrite will help it.

Again, we begin with the choppy writing

FIRST ATTEMPT

I decided to improve my writing. I just didn't know how.

A writer trying to combine the sentences with only a comma falls victim to the comma splice.

COMMA SPLICE

I decided to improve my writing, I just didn't know how.

It is important to remember this second method requires *both* a comma and a coordinating conjunction to correctly smooth choppy writing:

BETTER

I decided to improve my writing, *but* I just didn't know how.

Surf's up...

Comma splices in cyberspace!
This site shows you how to
avoid the dreaded comma splice:

http://grammar.ccc.commnet.edu/grammar/runons.htm

BRAIN TICKLERS
Set # 36

Use Method no. 2 to combine the following
simple sentences into a flowing sentence.

1. Eric is concerned about his writing skills.
    He does nothing to improve them.

2. I want to listen to the music. I can't
    because the baby is sleeping.

3. We went out to eat. Then, we went to a movie.

4. Janet was careless and forgetful. She lost her purse.

5. Bob and Helen decided to eat at the new restaurant. They invited Ann.

6. We were angry at all the traffic. We called the mayor's office.

7. Jason felt that both candidates were qualified. He chose not to vote on Election Day.

8. My grandmother wanted to visit me in Boston. She was afraid to leave her home.

Refer to page 177 for some
possible sentences.

Method no. 3: Let the comma and semicolon join forces

Choppy writing can also result from repeated phrases. Many writers, by repeating certain parts of sentences to provide the reader with facts or opinions, end up with a series of choppy, repetitious sentences. The third method of this chapter's technique frees your writing from repetitious wording by using a semicolon to link the repetitious short sentences and a comma to replace the repeating words. The following example shows the technique's method for eliminating choppy, repetitious sentences.

FIRST ATTEMPT

John elected to attend Stanford. Mary elected to attend Harvard.

Use a semicolon and a comma to combine the choppy sentences into a single sentence without losing any information.

BETTER

John elected to attend Stanford; Mary, Harvard.

Notice how the repetitious words, *elected to attend,* in the second sentence were eliminated. To make sure that you can use the Painless Technique's last method to improve your writing, work through the following exercise.

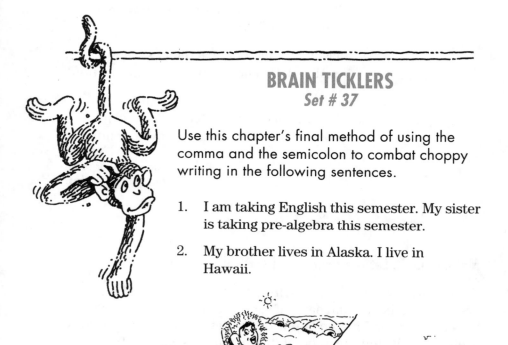

BRAIN TICKLERS
Set # 37

Use this chapter's final method of using the comma and the semicolon to combat choppy writing in the following sentences.

1. I am taking English this semester. My sister is taking pre-algebra this semester.

2. My brother lives in Alaska. I live in Hawaii.

3. Cassandra earned an A on her essay. John earned a B on his essay. Marsha earned a B on her essay.

4. We are traveling to Iceland this spring. We will be going to Bermuda this winter.

(Answers are on pages 177–178.)

This chapter's Painless Technique illustrates the different methods for using the comma to smooth out your writing by

1. creating introductory phrases

2. combining independent clauses

3. eliminating repetition

Surf's up...

Glide into this site for more information about using the powerful comma:

www.thepunctuationguide.com/comma.html

We learned how each method smoothes the choppy writing into flowing prose. To test your understanding of this chapter's Painless Technique, try the following exercise.

BRAIN TICKLERS
Set # 38

Apply this chapter's technique with its three methods to *Rachel's Dream*. Remember that your goal is to create a smoothly flowing paragraph.

Rachel's Dream

Rachel had never given much thought about what she was going to do when she grew up. She has now decided to become a writer. Creativity runs in her family. Her brother is a writer. Her sister is a screenwriter. Mr. Stones is her English teacher. He told her that she had a talent for writing. She responded by starting a writing journal. Now she is writing in it every day. Rachel is excited about writing a bestseller. She knows that she must work very hard to accomplish this dream.

Refer to page 178 for one possible revision.

Practice makes permanent

Using commas to make your writing flow will dramatically improve your writing style. As with all the other Painless Techniques, honing your new skill and making it a permanent part of your style should be your ultimate goal. Try the following, on a regular basis, to keep your technique sharp and part of your permanent writing style.

1. Using a previous writing assignment, examine it for comma misuse. Also, examine whether there are short, choppy sentences that could be combined into a longer, flowing sentence by using the methods of this chapter's Painless Technique.

2. Select a passage from an exciting book that you have read. Notice how the author used commas to create flowing sentences.

Creating readable rhythm

The techniques you mastered will add both power and grace to your writing. Now you should feel comfortable writing long, flowing sentences. The next chapter will further improve your writing by mixing these flowing sentences into a readable rhythm.

BRAIN TICKLERS—THE ANSWERS

Set # 33, page 159

1. compound
2. complex
3. simple
4. compound-complex

Set # 34, pages 164–165

1. Angered by Tim, Joe slammed down the telephone. (8)

2. Very embarrassed to participate in class, Mary answered a question for the first time yesterday. (15)

3. Interested in learning about toads, the students listened closely to their teacher. (12)

4. Excited at the thought of receiving presents, Jason stayed up all night and was the first one in the living room on Christmas Day. (24)

5. Depending upon the weather, we will leave tomorrow if it is close to being pleasant. (15)

6. Waiting to be fed, the baby is sitting in his high chair. (12)

7. Removed from society, the hermit had little use for contemporary technological advances. (12)

8. Having just won the Kentucky Derby, the young jockey now set her sights on the prestigious Preakness. (17)

Set # 35, page 167

1. After playing their hearts out in the first game, the team continued to play that way throughout the season.

2. After working hard, I won first place in the writing competition.

3. Against his better judgment, he bought the sailboat.

4. With a very long dialogue scene, the protagonist and antagonist opened the play.

5. After his parents waved good-bye to their son, he raced off to enjoy his newfound freedom as a college student.

6. Under different circumstances, Mr. Jones may have voted for the challenger rather than the current mayor.

7. With her English teacher accompanying Sarah, they left for the meeting with the principal at two o'clock.

Set # 36, pages 170–171

1. Eric is concerned about his writing skills, yet he does nothing to improve them.

2. I want to listen to the music, but I can't because the baby is sleeping.

3. We went out to eat, and then we went to a movie.

4. Janet was careless and forgetful, so she lost her purse.

5. Bob and Helen decided to eat at the new restaurant, and they invited Ann.

6. We were angry at all the traffic, and we called the mayor's office.

7. Jason felt that both candidates were qualified, but he chose not to vote on Election Day.

8. My grandmother wanted to visit me in Boston, yet she was afraid to leave her home.

Set # 37, pages 172–173

1. I am taking English this semester; my sister, pre-algebra.

2. My brother lives in Alaska; I, Hawaii.

3. Cassandra earned an A on her essay; John and Marsha, B's.

4. We are traveling to Iceland this spring; Bermuda, this winter.

Set # 38, page 174

Rachel had never given much thought about what she was going to do when she grew up, but she has now decided to become a writer. Creativity runs in her family. Her brother is a writer; her sister, a screenwriter. Mr. Stones, her English teacher, told her that she had a talent for writing. She responded by starting a writing journal, and now she is writing in it every day. Rachel is excited about writing a best-seller, but she knows that she must work very hard to accomplish this dream.

CHAPTER SEVEN

Add Rhythm to Your Writing

CHANGE YOUR PACE
TO KEEP THEM READING

A writing style characterized by sameness in sentence length, type, and structure produces a monotonous essay guaranteed to bore even the most receptive reader. Whenever you write with same-length sentences, particularly sentences that are all very long or very short, your reader loses interest. Long sentences drone on and cause readers to forget the first part of the sentence by the time they reach the sentence's end. Conversely, as we noted in the previous chapter, a composition riddled with short sentences reads like a grade school primer. To avoid this unhappy result, vary your pace throughout the composition by varying the length, type, and structure of your sentences.

Painless Technique

#7: Vary the Type, Length, and Structure of Your Sentences to Add Rhythm to Your Writing.

If you vary your writing's pace, you will give it the necessary rhythm to keep your readers reading, and the way to create this rhythm is by writing with sentences that vary in type, length, and structure. Before we discuss this chapter's Painless Technique, please take a few minutes to review the previous chapter's discussion of simple, compound, complex, and compound-complex sentences.

VARY SENTENCE LENGTH

If you calculated the average sentence length of a well-written essay, it would total between 12 and 15 words. You would also notice that the writer included some sentences that were much longer, and some sentences that were much shorter. By using sentences of varying lengths, you will weave simple, compound, complex, and compound-complex sentences together to tell your story.

Let us examine two methods for varying sentence length. The first method entails following a long compound or complex sentence with a punchy, short sentence. The example below demonstrates how varying the sentence length can improve a piece of writing.

College Bound

John's older brother planned for his college education like a general plans a beach assault. He left nothing to chance and tried thinking of every possible resource. He wanted to assure himself admission into the hallowed halls of Princeton. Sometimes, he thought he should join the army rather than enroll at that center of learning.

All of the sentences in this passage are nearly the same length. Consequently, the passage provides information, but not in a very interesting fashion. Let's see how we can improve *College Bound*.

BETTER

College Bound

John's older brother planned for his college education like a general plans a beach assault, leaving nothing to chance and thinking of every possible resource to assure himself admission into the hallowed halls of an Ivy League center of learning. On the other hand, he could join the army!

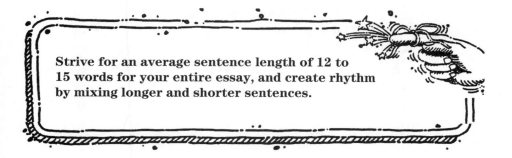

Strive for an average sentence length of 12 to 15 words for your entire essay, and create rhythm by mixing longer and shorter sentences.

Notice that the first sentence is 40 words long, whereas the second sentence is only 9 words long. The abrupt ending emphasizes the alternative career choice and creates an element of surprise. This method of interspersing a short sentence among long sentences is an easy way to add rhythm to your writing .

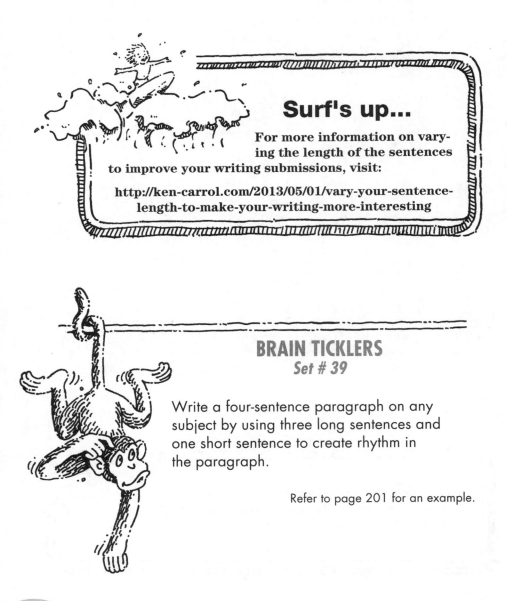

Surf's up...

For more information on varying the length of the sentences to improve your writing submissions, visit:

http://ken-carrol.com/2013/05/01/vary-your-sentence-length-to-make-your-writing-more-interesting

BRAIN TICKLERS
Set # 39

Write a four-sentence paragraph on any subject by using three long sentences and one short sentence to create rhythm in the paragraph.

Refer to page 201 for an example.

Notice how the following paragraph states information much as an encyclopedia does. By contrast, we know that we need to do more than merely state information if we want to keep our readers engaged.

The Athlete

Twenty years later, John took stock of his once sleek, muscled body. It was a body that had flowed so effortlessly up and down the basketball court. He had played basketball for four glorious years. His stomach now looked like he had swallowed a basketball. His hands ached with arthritis. He was winded after walking up a flight of steps.

Another way to add rhythm to your writing is to counterbalance a long opening sentence by following it with a series of short sentences. Let's see how that works with *The Athlete*.

BETTER

The Athlete

Twenty years later, John took stock of the once sleek, muscled body that had flowed so effortlessly up and down the basketball

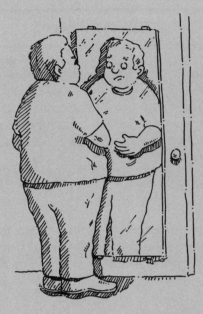

court for four glorious years. His stomach looked like he had swallowed a basketball. His hands ached with arthritis. Walking up a flight of steps winded him.

The opening sentence contains twenty-seven words, whereas the last three sentences each contain nine words or fewer. Notice how effectively the short sentences contrast and balance the opening sentence. Work through the following exercise to practice this sentence length varying technique.

BRAIN TICKLERS
Set # 40

Write a four-sentence paragraph on any subject using three short sentences and one long sentence to create rhythm in the paragraph.

Refer to page 201 for an example paragraph.

FRAGMENTS CAN CREATE RHYTHM

Using non-sentences or sentence fragments is another effective rhythm-generating technique. Inserting a sentence fragment can be an excellent way to make a point, especially when the fragment follows a long, complex sentence. Nevertheless, restrict your use of fragments to your creative writing pieces because they are out of place in a scientific paper.

Avoid using sentence fragments to help create rhythm in your writing if you suspect that your reader wants you to write with only complete sentences, even in creative pieces.

The following example demonstrates how using sentence fragments can add life to a passage. First, read the passage written with sentences of nearly equal length.

FIRST ATTEMPT

The Room

Mary slowly opened the door into the dark room. Fear was numbing her body and making it hard for her to concentrate. She wanted to run away from the dark room, but she could not make herself move. Taking a deep breath, she felt for the light switch next to the doorframe and flicked it. The light filled the once dark room and Mary looked everywhere, but she did not see anything.

The passage does not create the suspense the author desires. Fortunately, we can create suspense by writing with long, complex sentences and then slipping in a fragment at just the right moment.

BETTER

The Room

Mary slowly opened the door into the dark room. Fear was numbing her body and making it hard for her to concentrate. She

wanted to run away from the dark room, but she couldn't. Taking a deep breath, she felt for the light switch next to the doorframe and flicked it. Nothing.

Try the following exercise to help you use fragments to add rhythm to your writing.

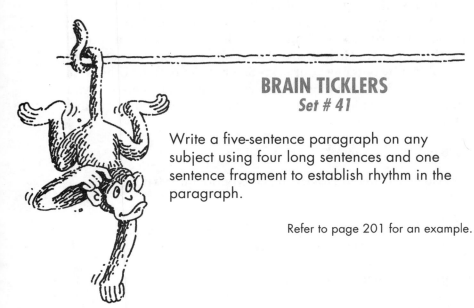

BRAIN TICKLERS
Set # 41

Write a five-sentence paragraph on any subject using four long sentences and one sentence fragment to establish rhythm in the paragraph.

Refer to page 201 for an example.

AVOID SENTENCES WRITTEN IN THE SAME FORM

Sameness with respect to sentence length and paragraph length is not the only villain responsible for monotonous writing. Sentences all written in the same form also create a boring passage. As we have seen, writing with only declarative sentences, especially short declarative sentences in the typical subject-verb-object form, will cause a reader's eyes to glaze over. The previous chapter's Painless Technique provided some methods to improve upon this type of writing. Now, let's examine another way we can correct this common writing fault.

Vary your sentence openings

The struggling writer rarely deviates from the standard subject-verb-object sentence form. Arguably, the majority of your sentences should be in this form because this style makes it easy to create a logical flow of events. However, as with sentence length, too many sentences written in the same form can lead to monotonous reading, but thankfully, this is an easy fault to correct.

Because the beginning often determines the sentence's form, become aware of the different ways to open sentences. Instead of starting every sentence with a noun used as a subject and then following it with a verb and object, delay introducing the subject by opening your sentence with something other than the subject. The following examples illustrate alternate forms of sentences available to combat the monotony created by endless left-to-right sentences.

Verb before the subject

Instead of writing the following conventionally structured sentences:

> Many students are in Ms. Webster's class.
> The semester is over today.

begin the sentences with a *verb*, so they now read:

> There *are* many students in Ms. Webster's class.
> Today *is* the end of the semester.

Open with an adverb

Instead of writing the following sentences in the typical subject-verb-object form:

> They sat silently as their writing teacher read their essays.
> The sun set quickly in the western sky.

begin them with an adverb:

> *Silently*, they sat as their writing teacher read their essays.
> *Quickly*, the sun set in the western sky.

Switch the noun and the direct object

Rather than composing sentences that lead off with the subject:

> Mary had seen the writing teacher this morning.
> The students placed their exams on the teacher's desk.

start the sentence with a *direct object*:

> *The writing teacher* was seen by Mary this morning.
> *The exams* were placed on the teacher's desk.

Remind yourself to use this method sparingly because this will create a sentence in the passive voice. Although passive voice sentences are fine, they take the action away from the subject, so use them only on occasion. If you need to review the passive voice, refer to Chapter Three.

Open with an adjective

Rather than writing the standard subject-verb-object sentence:

> She was angry and frustrated as she stared at the grade on her term paper.
> Maria felt overwhelmed as she continued working on her term paper.

begin the sentence with the *subject's modifying words*:

> *Angry* and *frustrated,* she stared at the grade on her term paper.

> *Overwhelmed,* Maria continued working on her term paper.

Lead with a prepositional phrase

Instead of introducing the sentence with the subject, *she*:

> She hoped the solution to her problem was in this classroom.

begin the sentence with a *prepositional phrase*:

> *In this classroom,* she hoped to find the solution to her problem.

Go with a gerund

Rather than writing the standard left-to-right sentence:

> Mary has a goal of writing well.

begin the sentence with a *gerund,* which is a noun made from a verb by adding *-ing.*

> *Writing* well is Mary's goal.

The preceding examples should provide you with some ideas for varying your sentence forms. Every so often, give standard left-to-right sentences a rest by substituting one of the above sentence forms in your writing. The following exercise asks you to practice this technique.

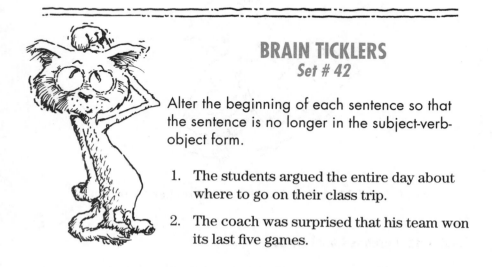

BRAIN TICKLERS
Set # 42

Alter the beginning of each sentence so that the sentence is no longer in the subject-verb-object form.

1. The students argued the entire day about where to go on their class trip.

2. The coach was surprised that his team won its last five games.

3. The students learned many of life's lessons in Mr. Greene's classroom.

4. The mother lovingly picked up her newborn baby.

5. The problem can be solved in a number of ways.

6. John likes to climb mountains and backpack.

7. He was upset that his story was not published, and so he quit writing.

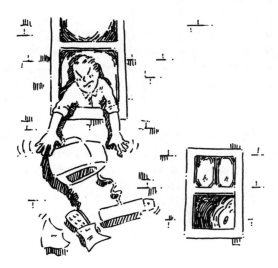

8. Martha is the best writer in the class.

9. The students enjoyed the guest speaker's stories about his travels abroad.

10. John had written the paper that earned him an A in less than 20 minutes.

Refer to page 202 for some possible revisions of these sentences.

Vary the kinds of sentences

The final way to add rhythm to your writing is to vary the types of sentences. We have seen how monotony sets in whenever you write sentence after sentence in the declarative. Although most of your sentences should be declarative, you should occasionally use other types of sentences; an occasional question, exclamation, or command is another way to relieve the declarative monotony. To understand what we are talking about, first read the following paragraph written with all declarative sentences.

FIRST ATTEMPT

Our class apprehensively waited for Ms. Martin to return our essays. She asked us to raise our hands if we thought we had done a good job writing our essay. She appeared surprised that no one raised his or her hand. She passed the papers back, and when she was finished, she raised her hand. She shouted that everyone had done a terrific job!

Next, read the following paragraph that breaks the above paragraph out of the purely declarative mode. Notice that by eliminating some of the declarative sentences, the writer is able to make use of dialogue.

BETTER

> Our class apprehensively waited for Ms. Martin to return our essays.
> "Raise your hand if you thought you did a good job on your essay," she commanded. "No one thinks he or she did a good job?"
> She passed the papers back, and when she was finished, she raised her hand and shouted, "I think everyone did a terrific job!"

Did you notice how the interrogative and exclamatory sentences deliver more snap to the paragraph? Nevertheless, be wary:

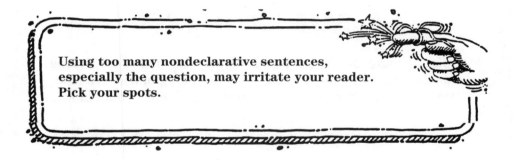

Using too many nondeclarative sentences, especially the question, may irritate your reader. Pick your spots.

The following exercise provides you with an opportunity to write a short passage using the above method.

BRAIN TICKLERS
Set # 43

Compose a multiple-paragraph passage. Occasionally use nondeclarative sentences throughout your passage.

Refer to page 202 for a sample passage.

PARAGRAPHS
CREATE RHYTHM TOO

Differing paragraph length also generates rhythm in your writing submission. For instance, a one-sentence paragraph such as the one in the following excerpt is a great way to make your point.

Forget Something?

College life was everything Mary had expected it to be: the mind-challenging courses, new friends, and of course, the odd professor or two, the oddest of whom was Dr. Freeman, her instructor for physics. By all accounts, he was a brilliant professor, but quite absent-minded. Last Tuesday, he was a few minutes into his lecture on angular momentum, when suddenly, his wife burst into the auditorium and interrupted him mid-sentence.

"You forgot your pants!"

    The following exercise provides an opportunity to create a rhythm with your paragraphs.

BRAIN TICKLERS
Set # 44

Write two or more paragraphs on any subject. Contrast the length of one of the paragraphs to add emphasis to your writing.

Refer to page 203 for a sample passage.

Talk to yourself and others

Look for ways to add rhythm to your writing by varying (1) the length of your sentences and paragraphs; (2) the openings of your sentences; and (3) the types of sentences. Your readers will appreciate the change of pace.

An excellent way to determine whether there is a rhythm to your writing submission is to read it aloud. If you are droning along as you read, use the technique of this chapter to give it some snap. Conversely, if it sounds great as you read aloud to yourself or your friends, you have done well. Try using this chapter's Painless Technique to add some rhythm to the bland paragraph on the next page. Remember to vary the length, the opening, and the type of the sentences.

BRAIN TICKLERS
Set # 45

Use the methods of this chapter's Painless Technique to provide some rhythm to the paragraph entitled *Stranded* below.

Stranded

This week of school was finally over. I was glad of that. I was now planning my well-deserved weekend. My best friend, Frank, wanted me to go with him to the beach. He said his brother would drive us to the beach in his 1989 Toyota. I had asked him if he was sure his car could even make it all the way across town. He said that he was sure it could make it to the beach, but he was not as confident that it would bring us home. I suppose there are worse places to be stranded than on the white beaches of Florida.

Refer to page 203 for a suggested paragraph.

Surf's up...

Surf into this site for more information on writing with rhythm:

http://www.dailywritingtips.com/
5-tips-about-writing-with-rhythm

Practice makes permanent

This chapter's Painless Technique is a simple but powerful one. Sentence after sentence and paragraph after paragraph of the same length and type will detract from your hard work. By learning this chapter's Painless Technique for adding rhythm to your writing, you will dramatically improve your submissions. As always, honing your new skill and making it a permanent part of your style should be your ultimate goal. Try the following, perhaps once a day, to keep this technique sharp.

1. Using a previous writing assignment, examine it for sentence sameness. Pull out a paragraph or two, and use your newly learned technique to make the excerpt flow better.

2. Pull some samples of your most recent writing. Calculate the average sentence length for a few paragraphs. Now, select an excerpt of what you feel is good writing. Calculate the excerpt's average sentence length. Any difference?

Adding some polish

The Painless Techniques that you have learned thus far will improve your writing, and you should notice this improvement. The next Painless Technique will polish your now strong writing by making you aware of some commonly misused words that detract from your work.

BRAIN TICKLERS—THE ANSWERS

Set # 39, page 184

The following passage makes use of a one-word sentence contrasted against three long sentences (20, 20, and 24 words, respectively.)

Vote

Vote. Why do Americans no longer exercise a right that people in other countries are willing to die for to achieve? Have we become too complacent about our civic duty, or rather, have we become too cynical about our elected leaders? The answer to these questions lies in the heart of each American; only when we search our hearts will we reaffirm this wonderful right.

Set # 40, page 187

The following passage opens with a 27-word sentence. This long sentence is then followed by three sentences containing 5 words each.

Our Earth

Caring for the environment is the most important duty we humans have because if we neglect this duty, there will be nowhere left for us to go. The ancient Greeks knew this. The conquering Romans knew this. The Native Americans knew this.

Set # 41, page 189

Time and Money

Time is money. This simple statement was true one hundred years ago, and it is true today. People have come to realize that they can exchange the services they can provide for money for the goods and services they need. There, the logic is undeniable; the more time a person has, the more opportunity he or she has to create valuable services. Many people avoid wasting money; however, these same people will waste time in nonproductive endeavors.

Set # 42, pages 192–193

1. On the subject of where to go on their class trip, the students argued the entire day.

2. By winning the last five games, the team surprised their coach.

3. In Mr. Greene's classroom, the students learned many of life's lessons.

4. Lovingly, the mother picked up her newborn baby.

5. Solving the problem can be done in a number of ways.

6. Climbing mountains and backpacking are what John likes.

7. Upset that his story was not published, he quit writing.

8. Of everyone in the class, Martha is the best writer.

9. Discussing his travels abroad, the guest speaker pleased the students with his stories.

10. In less than 20 minutes, John had written the paper that earned him an A.

Set # 43, page 196

Timing

Have you ever noticed how teachers always pick the worst times to assign projects and papers? My birthday is next week, and my parents want to throw a party for me.

My mother asked sweetly, "Why don't you invite some of your friends? But not more than six," she quickly added, as if ordering cupcakes.

I was so excited! I couldn't wait to go to school tomorrow.

The next morning, I raced into school and found my friends standing outside of our English teacher, Ms. Erickson's room. They didn't look very happy.

"Will you come to my party Saturday?" I asked the frowning group.

"We can't!" they screamed in unison. "We'll be working through the weekend on our English project."

I had completely forgotten about it. Guess what I'll be doing this weekend?

Set # 44, page 198

Notice how the second paragraph contrasts with the first paragraph full of long sentences.

Why Education?

Education provides the framework of our individual liberty. This is not just my opinion, but an everyday fact. It is so important for our children to learn the value of their education. Without education, they will never be able to realize their full potential.

Knowledge is power.

Set # 45, page 199

Stranded

Finally! This week of school was over! I was now planning a well-deserved weekend. My best friend, Frank, wanted me to go with him to the beach. His brother was going to take us there in his 1989 Toyota, he told me.

"Can his car even make it all the way across town?" I asked him.

"It can make it to the beach, but don't ask me about bringing us back."

Being stranded on the white beaches of Florida doesn't sound all that bad.

CHAPTER EIGHT

Gremlins in Your Writing

REPEAT OFFENDERS

Some writers consistently misuse certain words. Unfortunately, these words, when misused, detract from the authority and hard work of the author because the reader focuses on the writing mistake and ignores the writer's message. It's not fair, but it happens all too often. You can prevent this from occurring by using these commonly misused words properly.

Painless Technique

#8: Learn the Proper Usage of Commonly Misused Words.

THE TOP TEN GREMLINS

Below are the top ten gremlins, that is, the ten most commonly misused sets of words. To avoid bringing negative attention to your writing, make sure that you understand when to use them.

affect/effect
altogether/all together
infer/imply
lay/lie
disinterested/uninterested
sit/set
who/which/that
fewer/less
principal/principle
who/whom

Let's take a look at these potential writing destroyers.

Gremlin set no. 1: affect/effect

This first set of gremlins causes even the most careful writers to slip up once in a while. The verb *affect* means "to make an impression on, to influence." By contrast, the word *effect* can act as a noun or a verb. When acting as a noun, *effect* means "the result produced by a cause." When the word acts as a verb, it means "to cause or to bring about." Select the correct word in the examples below.

Poor writing will adversely _____ (affect, effect) your grade.

The coach slammed his hand on the table for _____ (affect, effect).

The rainstorm _____ (affected, effected) a delay in our arrival.

In the first sentence the author is telling us that poor writing will have a negative influence on your grade; therefore, we need to use *affect*, rather than *effect*. Similarly, in the second sentence, the coach is slamming his hand on the table to impress something upon the players; thus, *effect* is the proper word in this instance. Finally, in our last sentence, the consequence of the rainstorm is a late arrival. This means that we use *effected*, rather than *affected*.

CORRECT USE

Poor writing will adversely *affect* your grade.

The coach slammed his hand on the table for *effect*.

The rainstorm *effected* a delay in our arrival.

Gremlin set no. 2: altogether/all together

This is another gremlin couple that brings out the teacher's red correction pen, but once we understand their definitions, these words should not cause any trouble. *Altogether* means "completely, thoroughly." *All together* means "as a group." See if you can correctly use them in the following sentences.

Your answer in class was _____ (altogether, all together) wrong.

(Altogether, All together), the class answered the question incorrectly.

The first sentence is informing us that the answer was completely wrong; therefore, we need to use *altogether*. In the second sentence, the author states that, as a group, the class answered incorrectly. To write the sentence correctly, we must use *all together*.

CORRECT USE
Your answer in class was *altogether* wrong.

All together, the class answered the question incorrectly.

Another set of gremlins bites the dust! Pretty easy so far, right? But be careful—the next set can be tricky.

Gremlin set no. 3: infer/imply

The word *infer* means "to arrive at by reasoning" or "to deduce." Contrast this usage to the word *imply*, which means "to suggest or hint." Try your hand at the following sentences.

I _____ (implied, inferred) that I would have trouble passing the class when the teacher returned my exam with a red F on it.

I had _____ (implied, inferred) that I liked Mary Ellen, but I was too shy to do anything about it.

The first sentence is telling us that the student has deduced that he will have trouble passing the class because he earned an F on the midterm; therefore, we must use the word *infer* to get this point across. In the second sentence, the author is hinting that he liked Mary Ellen but was too shy to do anything about it; therefore, this sentence requires that we use *implied*.

CORRECT USE

I *inferred* that I would have trouble passing the class when the teacher returned my exam with a red F on it.

I had *implied* that I liked Mary Ellen, but I was too shy to do anything about it.

These sets of gremlins should not give you any trouble now, and you will be able to use them with confidence when you write. To make sure this is the case, complete the following exercise to apply what you have learned.

You should feel confident that you can keep these three sets of gremlins under control in your writing. Now let's move on to the fourth gremlin set.

BRAIN TICKLERS
Set # 46

Select the proper word for each of the following sentences.

1. We left (altogether, all together).

2. From his tone of voice, I (inferred, implied) that he was upset and angry.

3. How do the clouds (affect, effect) the temperature?

4. I felt (altogether, all together) out of place at the party on Saturday night.

5. The (inference, implication) taken from the fact that there are no school buses in front of school is that we will not be going on the class trip.

6. The Boy Scouts were not (affected, effected) by rain as they hiked through the hills of central Texas.

7. I am not (all together, altogether) sure why we are here.

8. Are you (inferring, implying) that I write poorly?

9. Such a statement could have a serious, long-term (affect, effect) on me.

(Answers are on page 223.)

Gremlin set no. 4: lay/lie

When to use *lay* or *lie* is relatively easy once you understand the definition of each word. To *lay* means "to put or place in a more or less horizontal position." Conversely, the phrase *to lie* means "to recline."

Most students know this, but they confuse themselves when they move away from the present tense. Listed below are the principal parts of these troublesome words:

Present	lay	lie
Past	laid	lay
Present Participle	laying	lying
Past Participle	laid	lain

Remember that *lay* requires a direct object; you always lay something. However, you never lie anything; you just *lie* down. Use the following two sentences to test your understanding.

Matt _____ (laid, lied) the blanket over the sleeping children.

Katie was _____ (laying, lying) on the new sofa.

In the first sentence, the subject, *Matt*, is placing the blanket in a horizontal position over the direct object, *the sleeping children*. Consequently, to write the sentence properly, we need to use the verb *laid*. In the next sentence, the subject, *Katie*, is reclining on the new sofa, which means that we must write the sentence with the verb, *lying*.

CORRECT USE

Matt *laid* the blanket over the sleeping children.

Katie was *lying* on the new sofa.

The next words are a particularly tricky set for some writers. Take your time, and make sure you understand when to use each word.

Remember, these examples are always here for your review. Let's take a look at them.

Gremlin set no. 5: disinterested/uninterested

The distinction between these two words eludes many writers. The word *disinterested* means "unbiased" or "neutral." By contrast, *uninterested* means "not interested" or "bored." The following two sentences will help you use these words correctly.

Ms. Smith was appointed as the judge for the trial because she was a _____ (disinterested, uninterested) party.

The football team was so far behind that it was _____ (disinterested, uninterested) in the halftime speech of its coach.

The writer means that Ms. Smith was appointed as a judge because she was unbiased, not because she did not care; therefore, we should describe Ms. Smith as a *disinterested* party. By contrast, the football team is not unbiased; it is aloof toward its coach. To properly describe the team's spirit, it is necessary to use *uninterested*.

CORRECT USE

Ms. Smith was appointed as the judge for the trial because she was a *disinterested* party.

The football team was so far behind that it was *uninterested* in the halftime speech of its coach.

Surf's up...

Check out this site to help you keep an annoying gremlin from ruining your writing:

http://grammarist.com/osage/ disinterested.uninterested/

We have almost finished. Now let's move on and tackle those pesky sit/set gremlins.

Gremlin set no. 6: sit/set

This is another word set that confuses students when they move from the present tense; therefore, we will examine the other tenses so that we are no longer confused. The principal parts of these two verbs are:

Present	sit	set
Past	sat	set
Past Participle	sat	set
Present Participle	sitting	setting

People *sit*, whereas you *set* something—with the following exceptions: the sun sets, concrete sets. Work through these two sentences.

Clara _____ (sat, set) at her usual place at dinner.

My brother is _____ (sitting, setting) the table for dinner.

Since Clara is a person, she *sits* at the table. In the first sentence, therefore, we must use *sat* rather than *set* to write the sentence properly. By contrast, the second sentence tries to describe the brother's action of preparing the table, and to do that he must place silverware and plates on the table. The verb that describes this action is the present participle, *setting*.

CORRECT USE
Clara *sat* at her usual place at dinner.

My brother is *setting* the table for dinner.

Surf's up...

There is help in cyberspace
if you need it to keep the
gremlins at bay:

www.getitwriteonline.com/archive/060602.htm

Before we move on, work through the following exercise to
make sure that you can correctly use these word sets.

BRAIN TICKLERS
Set # 47

Select the proper word for each sentence.

1. The competition became so boring
   that the (disinterested, uninterested)
   judge also soon became (disinterested,
   uninterested).

2. The dog (set, sat) on the car to keep
   warm.

3. I will just (lie, lay) the blanket down
   over here.

4. (Lie, lay) down on the bed in my room.

5. The Spirit Club arrived early to (set, sit)
   up the refreshments for the pep rally.

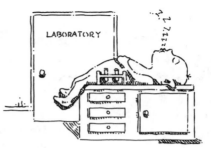

6. John was (lying, laying) asleep across the lab table.

7. (Sit, Set) down!

8. My brother is always (lying, laying) on the sofa.

9. The nurse had (lain, laid) a blanket over the shivering patient.

10. John was so (disinterested, uninterested) in the class that he fell asleep.

(Answers are on pages 223–224.)

Now we are ready to tackle some **triplet gremlins**. These confuse many writers, but by the time we have finished, you will never have a problem.

Gremlin set no. 7: who/which/that

Use the word *who* when you want to refer to people or to animals (that you want to personify). By contrast, use *which* to refer to animals or inanimate objects. Finally, you can use *that* to refer to either people or things.

I am the student _____ (which, who) signed up for the swimming lesson.

The food _____ (that, which, who) is sitting on the table is rotten.

The writer _____ (that, which, who) signed up for class is Jim.

Since *the student* obviously refers to a person, in the first sentence we must use the word *who* to refer to the student. In the following sentence, *the rotten pieces of food* are inanimate objects; therefore, we need to use the word *which* or *that* to refer to them. Finally, the subject, *writer*, in the third sentence is a person. This means that we need to use either *who* or *that* to refer to that person.

CORRECT USE

I am the student *who* signed up for the swimming lesson.

The food, *which* is sitting on the table, is rotten.

or

The food *that* is sitting on the table is rotten.

The writer *who* signed up for the class is Jim.

or

The writer *that* signed up for the class is Jim.

That was a rather difficult set, but this next set of gremlins should give you less problems—or is it fewer problems?

Gremlin set no. 8: fewer/less

Writers frequently misuse *fewer* and *less*. Let's examine these words and see when to use them. To begin, you should use *fewer* to refer to objects that can be counted, whereas *less* should be used to refer to qualities or concepts that cannot be counted. The following sentences will help with your understanding.

Mary received _____ (fewer, less) A's on her semester report card than you.

I suppose that is because I have _____ (fewer, less) determination.

Since Mary is able to count the number of A's on her semester report card, the writer should use *fewer* to describe the situation, rather than *less*. In the second sentence, because determination cannot be counted, the writer should not use *fewer.* Instead, *less* should be used to describe the amount of determination.

CORRECT USE

I received *fewer* A's on my semester report card than you.

I suppose that is because I have *less* determination.

The next set of gremlins confuses many writers, but it is very easy to choose correctly. Let's see how.

Gremlin set no. 9: principal/principle

The concept is a straightforward one. Use the word *principal* when referring to the principal of a school, the principal person in a movie, the principal cause, or the principal remaining on a loan. In contrast, the word *principle* means "rule or essential truth." Remember, we should live our lives by *principles*, and be respectful of the *principal* of the school. Test yourself with the sentences below.

"Work hard" is my guiding _____ (principal, principle).

The _____ (principal, principle) told me that I need to work harder.

In the first sentence, the writer is referring to a standard or a code for conducting her life; therefore, *principle* is the proper word to use. In the second sentence, a person is urging the writer to work harder, which means the writer must use *principal* to refer to this person.

CORRECT USE

"Work hard" is my guiding *principle.*

The *principal* told me that I needed to work harder.

One set to go! Unfortunately, it is a tough one for a lot of writers.

Gremlin set no. 10: who/whom

There are two main situations where these words occur. The first is where they begin subordinate clauses, and the other is where they begin questions. Let us first examine the subordinate clause situation.

In subordinate clauses, whether we use *who* or *whom* depends upon what the subordinate clause refers to. Use *who* if you are referring to the subject of the clause. Conversely, use *whom* if you are referring to the object of the clause. Try it for yourself.

The boys _____ (who, whom) failed the test did not study.

_____ (Who, Whom) are you driving to school?

Let's look at the first sentence. We must use *who* to begin the subordinate clause *failed the test* because we are referring to the subject of the sentence, *the boys*.

In the second sentence, the subject of the sentence is *you*. The person being driven is receiving the action and is, therefore, the object. This being the case, we must use *whom* in the sentence.

CORRECT USE

The boys *who* failed the test did not study.

Whom are you driving to school?

The rule regarding these words in questions is rather simple: If the question refers to the subject of the sentence, then choose *who*. If the question refers to the object of the sentence, then choose *whom*. The following examples illustrate this rule.

Who wrote this essay?

Notice that *who* refers to the subject of the sentence.

Whom does the article refer to?

Whom receives the referring; the article does the referring. Therefore, *whom* is correctly used here because it refers to the direct object.

Surf's up...

Here are a couple of sites that you can refer to so that your writing is gremlin-free:

http://www.grammar-monster.com/lessons/which_that_who.htm

web.ku.edu/nedit/whom.html

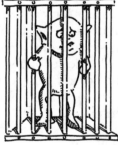

Those gremlins should be under control now; however, just to make sure they will not reappear, try the exercises below.

BRAIN TICKLERS
Set # 48

Choose the correct word in each of the following sentences.

1. The (principal, principle) reason we lost the game was my fumble at the one-yard line.

2. He had (fewer, less) bruises on his body than I did.

3. The author (which, who, that) wrote this book is very talented.

4. (Who/Whom) is your favorite author?

5. John, to (who/whom) I am related, is attending the class.

6. The (principal, principle) always attended every football game.

7. The (least, fewest) amount of time will be wasted if we walk rather than wait for the bus.

(Answers are on page 224.)

Practice makes permanent

Properly using these ten sets of word gremlins will keep your reader focused on the content of your writing. As with all the other Painless Techniques, honing your new skill and making it a permanent part of your style should be your ultimate goal. Try the following, on a regular basis, to keep your technique sharp and part of your permanent writing style.

1. Using a previous writing assignment, examine it for misuse of the ten problem sets of words.

2. Once a day, select a problem set and write a sentence or two using the words. Work your way through all ten sets, and then start over.

YOU HAVE STYLE, SUBSTANCE, AND GRACE

When properly employed, the eight techniques presented in this book will dramatically improve your writing, giving it a sense of style and grace. The last technique is a targeted technique. Its target is the dreaded essay.

BRAIN TICKLERS—THE ANSWERS

Set # 46, page 211

1. We left <u>all together</u>.

2. From his tone of voice, I <u>inferred</u> that he was upset and angry.

3. How do the clouds <u>affect</u> the temperature?

4. I felt <u>altogether</u> out of place at the party on Saturday night.

5. The <u>inference</u> taken from the fact that there are no school buses in front of school is that we will not be going on the class trip.

6. The Boy Scouts were not <u>affected</u> by rain as they hiked through the hills of central Texas.

7. I am not <u>altogether</u> sure why we are here.

8. Are you <u>implying</u> that I write poorly?

9. Such a statement could have a serious, long-term <u>effect</u> on me.

Set # 47, pages 215–216

1. The competition became so boring that the <u>disinterested</u> judge also soon became <u>uninterested</u>.

2. The dog <u>sat</u> on the car to keep warm.

3. I will just <u>lay</u> the blanket down over here.

4. <u>Lie</u> down on the bed in my room.

5. The Spirit Club arrived early to <u>set</u> up the refreshments for the pep rally.

6. John was <u>lying</u> asleep across the lab table.

7. <u>Sit</u> down!

8. My brother is always <u>lying</u> on the sofa.

9. The nurse had <u>laid</u> a blanket over the shivering patient.

10. John was so <u>uninterested</u> in the class that he fell asleep.

Set # 48, pages 220–221

1. The <u>principal</u> reason we lost the game was my fumble at the one-yard line.

2. He had <u>fewer</u> bruises on his body than I did.

3. The author <u>who</u> wrote this book is very talented.

4. <u>Who</u> is your favorite author?

5. John, to <u>whom</u> I am related, is attending the class.

6. The <u>principal</u> always attended every football game.

7. The <u>least</u> amount of time will be wasted if we walk rather than wait for the bus.

CHAPTER NINE

The Framework for Success

FIVE TYPES OF ESSAYS

This year may be the first time that you are asked to write an *essay* of any kind. Don't worry! Once you understand them, they are actually quite fun to write. So, let's get started. We'll begin with the basics. There are five types of essays:

- Argument
- Literary Analysis
- Explanatory
- Narrative
- Research

At first, this seems overwhelming, but it's really not because each of the essay types contains similar critical elements. Before we see what those are, let's see how each of the essay types are used.

Argument: The writer investigates a topic and forms an opinion on it. Next, the writer provides evidence and reasoning to support his or her position on that topic. The writer will typically present the opposite point of view and then provide evidence and reasoning against it.

Literary Analysis: The writer examines a work of literature and then explains how the author used plot, characters, setting, etc., to show the author's view on some aspect of life.

Explanatory: The writer presents a particular viewpoint or reports on an event or situation. This type of essay is similar to the Argument Essay, but it typically involves less research and is shorter in length.

Narrative: The writer tells a story from his or her perspective with the intent of illustrating some truth, lesson learned, or insight to the reader.

Research: The writer answers a question related to the topic he or she is studying.

As mentioned, all of the essay types have similar elements and requirements—that is to say, they have the same framework. This is good news! Master this framework and you will be on your way to becoming a successful essay writer!

First things first—Selecting a topic

Your teacher may assign your essay topic; however, if he or she allows you to choose your own topic, take note of the following guidelines. Selecting a proper topic is critically important. If you do this incorrectly, you will have a very difficult time writing your essay. Let's look at these helpful guidelines.

1. Select a narrow enough topic

Make sure that the topic you are considering is narrow enough to adequately discuss within the length of the essay your teacher has assigned. For instance, if you are assigned a two-page essay, the topic of *immigration* would be much too broad; rather, you might want to select how the immigration process affected your parents.

2. Availability of materials

Make sure the topic you are considering has an adequate amount of reference material readily available or you have enough personal knowledge to write the essay. The available reference material should include sources from recently published books, recent articles from scholarly magazines, and information from currently updated web sites hosted by universities or similar scholarly institutions.

Note: Keep a good record of the reference materials that you use or plan to use so that you will be able to properly cite, when necessary. We'll discuss citing reference material later in this chapter.

3. Level of complexity of the topic

The topic you are considering should challenge you, rather than overwhelm or confuse you. You won't impress your teacher by turning in an essay full of information and ideas that he or she knows you do not understand. As you will see, no matter what type of essay you are writing, you must not only provide facts about your topic, but you must also analyze those facts. An overly difficult topic will not allow you to fulfill both of these requirements. Similarly, do not choose a topic that is below your understanding level because one of the purposes of being assigned the essay is for you to learn more about a topic that interests you.

4. What is the rest of the class doing?

Take note of what your classmates are considering for their topics. Be different. Your teacher will appreciate reading something different and the fact that you are the one providing it. Discuss the topic you are considering with your parents or other adults who will give you an honest opinion, and whose tastes may be fairly close to those of your teacher.

Surf's up...

The following site discusses how to pick an essay topic:

www.canuwrite.com/essay_topic.php

Now that you have your topic, you are ready to move on to the basic structure of an essay.

THE BASIC STRUCTURE
OF AN ESSAY

Because all essays have similar structures, writers can utilize the same process for writing an essay, no matter what type. Let's look at the basic structure of an essay and its three components, which are:

1. One Introductory Paragraph;
2. Two or more Body Paragraphs; and
3. One Concluding Paragraph.

The Introductory Paragraph

The job of the Introductory Paragraph in any type of essay is twofold: 1) describe generally your essay's topic; and 2) inform your reader what you would like to convince them of about your topic. The first few sentences of the Introductory Paragraph should introduce your reader to the topic. Following these sentences, all introductory paragraphs should conclude with a **Proposition Statement**. It is with the Proposition Statement that you explain to your reader what you would like to convince him or her about the topic. We'll talk more about the Proposition Statement in a bit.

The Body Paragraphs

Your essay will usually contain two to five Body Paragraphs depending on the required length of the essay. The purpose of the Body Paragraphs is to develop your essay so that it is interesting and informative to read. Each Body Paragraph should be focused on only one item or concept directly related to the topic and the Proposition Statement. That means every sentence in the paragraph should be related to the other sentences in the paragraph, and each sentence should flow from the preceding sentence. Whenever you achieve this, your essay is said to have **unity**, and that is a good thing!

Each Body Paragraph should end with a sentence that restates the focus of the paragraph and transitions to the next paragraph. Refer to Chapter 5, where we learned about transitioning between sentences in paragraphs and transitioning between paragraphs. With certain types of essays, such as Argument Essays and Research Essays, the Body Paragraphs will contain parenthetical citations that refer to the reference materials that you used to write your essay.

The Concluding Paragraph

Concluding Paragraphs should not merely restate the Proposition Statement but should readdress it in light of the evidence, reasoning, and narrative in your essay. *The Concluding Paragraph should not present any new material*, and it generally should be shorter than the Body Paragraphs.

Now that we understand the basic structure of any essay, we can develop a process for writing any type of essay. We are going to use the POWER template!

THE *POWER* TEMPLATE

Once you have narrowed your research down to choose a topic (or it has been chosen for you), it is time to use the POWER template to begin constructing your essay. The POWER template is this chapter's Painless Technique. Obviously, creating a quality essay requires effort, but this template will help you to be efficient with your effort.

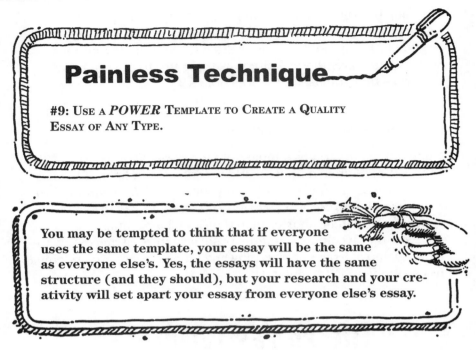

Painless Technique

#9: USE A *POWER* TEMPLATE TO CREATE A QUALITY ESSAY OF ANY TYPE.

You may be tempted to think that if everyone uses the same template, your essay will be the same as everyone else's. Yes, the essays will have the same structure (and they should), but your research and your creativity will set apart your essay from everyone else's essay.

The Proposition Statement

We begin with the letter "P," the first letter in the POWER template. Once you have selected a topic, write a one-sentence statement that establishes what you want to convince your reader of concerning your topic. This sentence is known as a ***Proposition Statement***. Its purpose is to give your essay a definite plan and strategy, and as mentioned earlier, it should be the <u>last sentence</u> in your Introductory Paragraph. It is critically important to write a Proposition Statement, and it is critically important that it be only one sentence. If you cannot explain what you hope to convince your reader of in one sentence, you probably do not have a clear idea of what you want to write about.

As you embark on your research and preliminary thinking, you may find that you need to revise your Proposition Statement in light of your research and/or new ideas. This process of researching, thinking, and revising is necessary for establishing how you will properly fill in the structure of your essay. If your essay requires research, make sure you do the research. This work in the beginning of the process will make writing the essay much easier.

Once you have selected a Proposition Statement, ask your-self whether it interests you or informs you enough to go further. Obviously, if it doesn't intrigue or inform you, it probably will not intrigue or inform your teacher either. As a further check, ask your parents or some other adults; notice how they react to your proposition statement. Now let's look at how to create a **winning Proposition Statement** for each type of essay.

Let's begin with the *Argument Essay*.

Example 1: The Argument Essay

Earlier in this chapter, we learned that the purpose of an Argument Essay is to investigate a topic and then form an opinion on it. You then provide evidence and reasoning to support your claim. Similarly, you will want to introduce the opposing claim and then show through evidence and reasoning that it is not as strong as your claim.

Suppose you are writing an Argument Essay that you have titled *Helping Students Retain What They Have Learned.* In it you want to convince your reader that it would be in the best interests of students to attend school year-round. Let's look at some possible Proposition Statements.

Argument Essay—*Helping Students Retain*
What They Have Learned

FIRST ATTEMPT
Students forget a lot of what they learn in school.

This is not a good Proposition Statement because it is too broad, and it will not provide your reader any idea of what you are really going to discuss in the essay or what you are trying to convince him or her.

Students forget much of what they learned during the school year over their annual summer vacations; therefore, the solution to this problem is to attend school year-round.

Notice how this Proposition Statement explains exactly what you will be discussing in your essay and your position on it. Notice that this Proposition Statement is not merely a statement of fact; rather, it states a fact but then makes a statement related to that fact that someone could agree or disagree with.

The next type of essay is the ***Literary Analysis Essay***. Let's work on a Proposition Statement for this essay type.

Example 2: The Literary Analysis Essay
In the Literary Analysis Essay, you examine a piece of literature and analyze it to show how the author used the elements of the work to express the author's view on some aspect of life. Typically, you will be asked to read a book or story, and your teacher will ask you to analyze the work with the idea of interpreting the author's message and purpose in writing the work.

Suppose you want to develop a Proposition Statement for a Literary Analysis Essay entitled *What The Right Stuff Can Teach Us*. Let's see how to do that.

Literary Analysis Essay—
What The Right Stuff Can Teach Us

Tom Wolfe's <u>The Right Stuff</u> is about the ordeals and adventures of the seven men selected to be America's first astronauts.

This is a poor Proposition Statement for a Literary Analysis Essay. Although it is factually correct, it is a mere summation of the novel, not an analysis of some aspect of it. This is the most common mistake students make when asked to write a Literary Analysis Essay. Rather than analyze the story, they write a summation. Analyze! Don't Summarize!

BETTER

In <u>The Right Stuff</u>, Tom Wolfe uses his main characters—the first seven Mercury astronauts selected by NASA in 1959—to show us how these men, thrust into a pressure cooker situation to beat each other to be the first American into space, responded not by trying to defeat each other but by striving for their own personal excellence, which in turn enabled the entire group to excel beyond all expectations.

This Proposition Statement is much better. It informs the reader that the topic is harmless competition and how author Tom Wolfe shows how a person can improve himself or herself without sacrificing the needs of the group.

We now have a Proposition Statement for our ***Literary Analysis Essay***. Let's move on to the ***Explanatory Essay***.

Example 3: The Explanatory Essay

As mentioned earlier, an Explanatory Essay presents a particular viewpoint or explains an event or situation. These essays are less formal than the Research Essay, so they require much less outside research, if any. Let's suppose you are writing an Informative Essay, *What's So Great About Exercising?* You will need a Proposition Statement.

Explanatory Essay—
What's So Great About Exercising?

FIRST ATTEMPT

A healthy lifestyle is a good goal to achieve.

This is a poor Proposition Statement because it is broad, it is uninformative, and it is uninteresting.

BETTER

Regular daily exercise benefits people by improving their cardiovascular and muscular systems, by improving their emotional outlook, and by helping them sleep better.

Notice how this Proposition Statement is much narrower and provides the reader a clear understanding of what the essay is about and the writer's viewpoint on it. This statement also allows the writer to use one body paragraph for each of the three ways that exercise benefits people.

Let's move on to the ***Narrative Essay***.

Example 4: The Narrative Essay

Whenever you write a Narrative Essay, you tell a story from your perspective with the intent of illustrating some truth or insight to your reader. The Proposition Statement of a Narrative Essay plays a slightly different role from that of one in an Argument Essay or an Exposition Essay in that it usually begins with the events of a personal story and then identifies a theme that connects the personal story to a life lesson.

Suppose you are writing a Narrative Essay entitled *Never Again*. You will need a Proposition Statement for your Introductory Paragraph.

Narrative Essay—*Never Again*

FIRST ATTEMPT

Preparation when going on a trip is important.

You should be able to see by now that this is a poor Proposition Statement. Why? Because it is so broad that it provides the reader with no idea of what the writer experienced and how that experience changed the writer's life.

BETTER

I'll never again head off on a trip with no money, with no phone, and without telling anyone where I am going.

Here, the writer has narrowed the essay down to a story about a *personal* trip and how his lack of preparation caused him problems. It will be easy now for the writer to show how the events of the story demonstrate the life-changing lesson that he learned.

Finally, let's look at the last type of essay—the *Research Essay*.

Example 5: The Research Essay

The purpose of the Research Essay is to allow the writer to answer a question related to the topic he or she is studying and researching.

Below, let's assume that you have researched what happens whenever certain schools replaced unhealthy foods with healthy ones in their cafeterias. The title of your Research Essay is: *Is Serving Healthy Foods in Schools Effective?* Let's look at some possible Proposition Statements.

Research Essay—*Is Serving Healthy Foods
in Schools Effective?*

FIRST ATTEMPT

Some schools started serving healthy foods at lunch.

This Proposition Statement, although factual, provides your reader with no clue as to what you have researched. More importantly, it provides no question that your research can answer in the essay. Notice how the following Proposition Statement answers the question: Do students eat the healthy foods that have replaced the unhealthy foods?

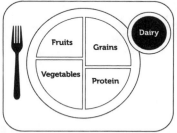

BETTER

After a relatively short period, students began eating the healthy foods introduced by the school.

That is the first step of the template. It's an important one because if you select a good Proposition Statement, the rest of the steps in the template will be easier to complete.

BRAIN TICKLERS
Set # 49

Below are five possible Proposition Statements, one for each type of essay. Determine if each is a suitable Proposition Statement. If not, rewrite it to make it so. Feel free to add facts as necessary.

1. Wearing a helmet while riding a bike is a good idea. *(Research Essay)*

2. In Poe's narrative poem, *The Raven*, the raven symbolizes the fate no human can escape—death. *(Literary Analysis Essay)*

3. I will never again tell my sister a secret. *(Narrative Essay)*

4. There are some good ways to relieve stress. *(Explanatory Essay)*

5. To keep young people from taking up smoking, athletes and entertainment artists should speak out against it. *(Argument Essay)*

(Answers are on page 258.)

If necessary, modify your Proposition Statement

As your essay develops and you focus your topic, test the Proposition Statement against what you have written so far. If necessary, modify your Proposition Statement as your research or any new ideas indicate.

Once you are satisfied with your Proposition Statement, you are ready to move to the next section of the template: the outline.

Creating the Outline

The "O" in POWER represents "Outline." Once you have constructed your essay's Proposition Statement, you are ready to create a preliminary outline containing your main points that will support your Proposition Statement. Each of these main points should be the focus of one Body Paragraph.

Let's see how this works with our first example, the *Argument Essay*: *Helping Students Retain What They Have Learned.* Our Proposition Statement for this essay was:

> Students forget much of what they learned during the school year over their annual summer vacations; therefore, the solution to this problem is to attend school year-round.

Below is the start of our outline. Notice that each Body Paragraph addresses one aspect of the topic and should support the essay's Proposition Statement in the Introductory Paragraph.

Argument Essay—*Helping Students Retain What They Have Learned*

- I.   Introductory Paragraph
- II. Results of Various Studies
- III. Why Students Forget
- IV. Students Need a Break and Family Time
     [contrary argument]
- V.   Concluding Paragraph

This is a good start. Now we want to build our outline from the research we have done. Notice how the outline sets out three main points that comprise the headings of the POWER outline. Depending on the length of your essay, you should have two to three main points (headings) for shorter essays, and you should have three to five main points (headings) for longer essays. Remember, all essays must begin with an Introductory

Paragraph, which will always be our first heading. Similarly, all essays must end with a Concluding Paragraph, which in our example will be Heading V.

Because this is an Argument Essay, we will be citing references to provide evidence to support our Proposition Statement. We will need to cite those references in a shorthand manner in the body of the essay (*parenthetical citations*) and then more formally at the end of the essay (*full citations*). It is a good idea to mention your references in your outline. That way, when you begin writing, you will know when to insert your information from the reference material.

Let's continue to build our outline for this essay. You want to do this because the more detailed you make your outline, the easier it will be to write your essay. This is because you will have organized everything that you want to write in your essay.

Argument Essay—*Helping Students Retain What They Have Learned*

I. Introductory Paragraph
II. Results of Various Studies
   A. Forget 30% (Lopez)
   B. Forget nearly 50% (Smith)
   C. Personal experiences
III. Why Students Forget
   A. Mind "switches gears"
      1. Moves from academics to leisure (Smith)
   B. School knowledge crowded out
      1. Video games
      2. Television
   C. Waste of students' time and taxpayer money

IV. Students Need a Break and Family Time [Contrary Argument]
   A. Young people are not adults
      1. No ill effects from all-year schooling (Lopez)
      2. Continue to see their school friends (Smith)
   B. Summer allows for family experiences and bonding
      1. Maintain summer vacation, but shorten to three weeks
      2. Actually less strain on the family (Smith)
V. Concluding Paragraph

Works Cited

You will list your references in full citation form here. We will discuss proper citation format later in this chapter.

We can proceed through the same process to outline our Example 2, **Literary Analysis Essay**, entitled *What The Right Stuff Can Teach Us Today*. This essay's Proposition Statement was:

In The Right Stuff, Tom Wolfe uses his main characters—the first seven Mercury astronauts selected by NASA in 1959—to show us how these men, thrust into a pressure cooker situation to beat each other to be the first American into space, responded not by trying to defeat each other but by striving for their own personal excellence, which in turn enabled the entire group to excel beyond all expectations.

Although we don't do any outside research for a Literary Analysis Essay, it is extremely important to back up your claims and opinions that you asserted in the body of your essay with examples from the text of the literary work. Our essay might outline as follows. The numbers in parentheses are the page number where the idea or event can be found.

Literary Analysis Essay—
What The Right Stuff Can Teach Us

I.   Introductory Paragraph
II. Only One Man Can Be The First (114)
   A. Made themselves better
   B. Ann Glenn example (262–263)
III. Bore Ridicule of Fellow Test Pilots in Silence
   A. Didn't respond with words
   B. Gordon Cooper answers in deed (341–344)
IV. Concluding Paragraph

In Example 3, we were writing the **Explanatory Essay**—*What's So Great About Exercising?* Typically, in an Explanatory Essay, the Proposition Statement will contain the points that you want to develop in your Body Paragraphs. Our Proposition Statement for this essay was as follows:

Regular daily exercise benefits people by improving their cardiovascular and muscular systems, by improving their emotional outlook, and by helping them sleep better.

Typically, an Explanatory Essay will be shorter in length than an Argument Essay and not involve as much research, if any. So, our outline could look as follows:

Explanatory Essay—
What's So Great About Exercising?

I. Introductory Paragraph
II. Improved Cardiovascular and Muscular Systems
    A. Improved blood pressure and pulse readings
    B. Stronger, yet more flexible
III. Improved Emotional Outlook
    A. Sense of well-being
    B. Runner's high
IV. Better Sleep
    A. Brain health
    B. Weight loss
V. Concluding Paragraph

Next, we move to Example 4, the **Narrative Essay**—*Never Again.* In this Narrative Essay, the writer tells a personal story with the intent of illustrating some life lesson learned. Although Narrative Essays are more story-like, they still follow the same basic outline structure. Notice that the outline is quite detailed.

Narrative Essay—
Never Again

I. Introduction
II. Headed to Fishing Cabin
    A. No preparation
    B. Didn't tell anyone
    C. On the road for thirty minutes
III. The Breakdown
    A. No other cars around
    B. No food or water
IV. The Police Rescue
    A. My worried friend
    B. My frantic parents
V. Conclusion

Finally, we move to Example 5, the **Research Essay**, entitled *Is Serving Healthy Foods in Schools Effective*? Recall that our Proposition Statement for this essay was:

> After a relatively short period, students begin eating the healthy foods introduced by the school.

Remember, we do not only want to show the results of our research in our Research Essay, but we also want to answer our *research question*. Notice the level of detail in a Research Essay outline. Take note, also, of the reference material noted in parentheses.

Research Essay—*Is Serving Healthy Foods in Schools Effective?*

I. Introductory Paragraph
II. Several Dozen School Districts Have Drastically Changed Their Menus
    A. French fries have been replaced by vegetables and fruit selections (Villarreal)
    B. Bottled water instead of soft drinks and sports drinks in vending machines (Whitaker)
III. Survey of the Students' Reaction
    A. The first week
        1. 65% left on shelves or thrown away (Amato)
    B. What happened over time?
        1. University of Texas (Amato)
            a. Sales of healthy foods steadily improved
        2. Cornell University results (Brinkman)
            a. Same result
IV. Where Are These School Districts Months Later?
    A. Sales of healthy foods are up (Villarreal)
    B. Effect on the rest of the family
V. Concluding Paragraph

Works Cited

As with the Argument Essay, your reference information will be fully cited in this section.

Now we have seen how to outline each of the five types of essays. Outlining is critically important to essay writing. If your outline is well thought out and detailed, the essay almost writes itself. Many students mistakenly believe that they can skip this process to save time. However, omitting the outline step costs them time spent in wasted research and, more importantly, doing so ultimately lowers the quality of their essay.

If you feel you need more help, check out the following web site.

Surf's up...

The following site continues the discussion on outlining:

www.teachervision.com/writing/essays/1779.html

Do not trash your template

This chapter's Painless Technique is a very simple but powerful one; however, it is only powerful if you use it. As you work through the research process, make sure your thinking and research are supporting your main points. Don't let inadequate research or hurried thinking force you to change your outline. You can avoid this unfortunate situation by starting early on your essay so that you have enough time for research or thinking through your narrative story. On the other hand, don't be afraid to change your outline if your research and thought process make it necessary. Your outline is a preliminary one, and your research and thought process may direct you to modify or replace some of your points. Once your outline is framed up, it is time to move on to the next section of the template.

The rough draft: get those ideas on paper

The "W" in POWER stands for "Write." Once you have your Proposition Statement and detailed outline, it should be an easy task to write a rough draft of your essay. Write the first draft with content in mind, rather than concentrating on style. Get your thoughts down on paper! Remember to always keep checking to see if the rough draft fits your Proposition Statement and the main points of your outline.

Let's see how this part of the template works for our example essays. We'll begin with the ***Argument Essay***.

Argument Essay—*Helping Students Retain*
What They Have Learned

Parents, educators, politicians, and students themselves all agree that education is vital to the success of the individual and vital to the success of this country. By definition, education is a progression of learning. However, in this country, it is not a smooth progression; rather, it is a series of progressions and regressions—significant regressions. Students forget much of what they have learned during the school year over their annual summer vacations; therefore, the solution to this problem is to attend school year-round.

Various educational groups have conducted studies to identify and quantify this problem. One such study by the University of California showed that students forgot more than thirty percent of what they learned during the preceding school year over summer vacation (Lopez). Similarly, a University of Texas study showed the knowledge lost was nearly half (Smith). With my own personal experience, I know that I need to review much of the math that I learned the previous school year after I return to school from summer vacation.

Why do students forget? The studies show their mind "switches gears" from academics to what is going on around them, namely, leisure activities (Smith). What are these leisure activities? For most children, these activities are video games and television. Neither one is conducive to the retention of academic knowledge. The result is that much of the time spent in school during the previous academic year was wasted. This is a waste of the students' time and taxpayer money.

Wait! You may say, "Young people are not adults. They can't work year-round. They need a break from school." The studies do not support this. Many European countries and Asian countries have school year-round, and the students show no ill effects (Lopez). Furthermore, in pilot programs in this country where the students attend school all year, the vast majority of students enjoy it more than having a long summer vacation because they get to continue to see their school friends (Smith). What about family life then? Isn't summer the time for family experiences and bonding? That is certainly true, but most families don't want to, or can't afford to, take a three-month vacation. The solution: Send the students to school year-round, but give them three weeks, rather than three months, of vacation during the summer. In a recent poll, 80 percent of the parents questioned said they would prefer that because it would save on child care, and it was actually less strain on the family because the children weren't around as much (Smith).

The time has come for year-round school with a three-week summer vacation. It solves the problem of students forgetting much of what they have learned the previous year, while at the same time giving families a chance to do things together in the summer.

Works Cited

Lopez, Adrianna. *Students' Minds on Summer Vacation.* University of California, Berkeley, Sept. 2014 Web. 28 Apr. 2015.

Smith, Justin. *The Effect of Summer Vacation on Middle and High School Students; A Survey.* Texas U, Aug 2014 Web. 23 Apr. 2015.

That was our first draft of our *Argument Essay*. Let's see how a first draft of the *Literary Analysis Essay* might turn out.

Literary Analysis Essay—
What The Right Stuff Can Teach Us

The world we live in is a competitive one. As individuals, we must compete against other individuals for resources, employment, and a path for a future. This relentless competition can make our world not a nice place to live in sometimes. Is there a way to help us cope? In The Right Stuff, Tom Wolfe uses his main characters—the first seven Mercury astronauts selected by NASA in 1959—to show us how these men, thrust into a pressure cooker situation to beat each other to be the first American into space, responded not by trying to defeat each other but by striving for their own personal excellence, which in turn enabled the entire group to excel beyond all expectations.

Wolf makes it clear from the outset that the seven men were keenly aware that only one of them could be the first American in space. Only one of them could be the first American to orbit Earth (114). Being the first brought the glory. No one would ever remember who was second. Yet, Wolf shows how they, individually and collectively, refused to sabotage each other. Rather, each man chose to make himself the best astronaut he could be and the best team member he could be. Yes, they competed mightily against each other, but they stood firm as a group. When John Glenn protected his stuttering wife, Anne, from the press, publicity-happy NASA officials wanted to force him to make her hold press conferences, but they knew they couldn't because "on something like this, the seven would stand against them like an army" (262–263).

They bore the ridicule of their fellow test pilots, who taunted them that a monkey had done their job (162). Not only was it was hurtful, but it was also somewhat true. They refused to answer with words, but they did respond in action. Although his space suit was dangerously malfunctioning, Gordon Cooper landed his damaged space capsule within four miles of the recovery ship after its automated control system had shorted out (341–344).

They were indeed the Brotherhood of the Right Stuff, not because they were daring and brave; a lot of men before them and after them were that. Rather, they understood the importance of self; but, more importantly, they understood the importance of the group. They were individuals who acted as a body of one, not a body of individuals. We would do well to emulate them.

Next up is the ***Explanatory Essay***. Let's look at a possible rough draft for this essay.

Explanatory Essay—
What's So Great About Exercising?

Do you hate to exercise? I used to until I found out what I was missing. Regular daily exercise benefits people by improving their cardiovascular and muscular systems, by improving their emotional outlook, and by helping them sleep better.

Once a person begins exercising, he or she will almost immediately notice improvements in the cardiovascular system. If a person had high blood pressure, exercise can bring it down. Aerobic exercise will help lower your pulse rate, which means your heart doesn't have to work as hard. Exercising will help your muscular system by making you stronger, and at the same time, more flexible.

Not only does exercise physically improve you, but it also improves your emotional outlook on life. People who exercise will tell you that they have this sense of well-being. Who has not heard of a runner's high? It's that good feeling you get during a run.

Exercise not only helps you when you are awake, but it also helps you when you are sleeping. Once I started exercising, I slept much better. Good sleep is necessary for brain health, and it also aids in weight loss.

I am glad that I started exercising because I experienced those benefits of exercise almost immediately. If you don't exercise, give it a try. If you do, keep it up.

We are making great progress! Below is a possible first draft for the ***Narrative Essay***.

Narrative Essay—*Never Again*

Have you ever done something that you have regretted—I mean, really regretted? Well, I have, and I have learned my lesson. I will never again head off on a trip with no money, with no phone, and without telling anyone where I am going.

This happened after my freshman year at college. I had been home for only a few days, and a high school friend of mine called me. He told me he was heading to his fishing cabin up in the mountains, and he invited me to join him. I remembered good times at that cabin over the years, and so I immediately said, "Sure. I'm leaving now." The cabin was about an hour drive from my house. My parents weren't home, but I figured I would call them later and let them know what was going on. I grabbed a gym bag and stuffed some clothes into it, jumped into my car, and headed north.

Thirty minutes and thirty miles into the trip—exactly halfway there—the "check engine" light came on, and a few seconds later the car died. It took me less than a few seconds to realize I was in the middle of nowhere with no phone, with no money, and with no one knowing where I was. Well, I thought to myself, I'll flag down someone driving by and ask for help. I stood by my car for over two hours. Not a single car drove by. Now it was getting dark.

I figured I would be spending the night out on the road. I was not looking forward to that because I had not packed any food or water. Another hour passed, and my thoughts had turned gloomy. Then I saw flashing lights coming toward me. The police car pulled up beside me. "You're John, right?" the officer asked through the open window. I nodded, and before I could ask how he knew, the officer said, "Your friend called your parents. He was worried about you. Your parents called us. They were past frantic." Although I was happy—extremely happy—to be rescued, my heart was sinking. My mom is a worrier, and my dad has a heart condition. I felt rotten about putting them through all this.

As the officer pulled up to the house, Mom and Dad rushed out. I ran toward them, and before they could say anything, I said, "I will never do that again, ever." Then they both hugged me.

It's true, isn't it? By using the POWER Template, these essays almost write themselves! We can now move on to our last essay, the **Research Essay**.

Research Essay—*Is Serving Healthy Foods in Schools Effective?*

For the past two years, school cafeterias have been under pressure from parents, politicians, and teachers to include healthy foods and get rid of the junk food, fried food, and food high in trans fat (Whitaker). A few schools have done just that. The question is: How have the students reacted to the change? After all, if they refuse to eat the healthy foods, the school district has wasted taxpayer money and you have a bunch of hungry kids. Fortunately, my research shows this to not be the case. After a relatively short period, students began eating the healthy foods introduced by the school.

Several dozen school districts throughout the United States have drastically changed their menu over the past year (Villarreal). Most of these schools have replaced French fries and other fried foods with vegetables and fruit selections (Villarreal). One school district in Texas banned the sale of soft drinks and high-fructose sports drinks from vending machines (Whitaker). Bottled water replaced the soft drinks and sport drinks, and it was sold at very inexpensive prices (Whitaker).

How did the students react to the change? All of the school districts making the change compiled their own surveys, and many shared their data with local universities, which then compiled all of the data received. According to a study published by the University of Texas at Austin, during the first week, over 65 percent of the healthy substitutes were either left on shelves or thrown away, either uneaten or partially eaten (Amato). Although most programs got off to a bad start, nearly all of the programs experienced the same results over the next few weeks. The students increasingly began to purchase the healthy food, and the amount of healthy food thrown away steadily decreased over the same period. This trend was verified by two separate university studies—one at the University of Texas (Amato) and one done by Cornell University (Brinkman).

What is the status of these test programs months later? Nearly all report sales of the healthy food at about the same level as the unhealthy foods before the change (Villarreal). Furthermore, it appears that students exposed to healthy foods at school have asked for them at home (Simpson). This was a totally unexpected, but happy, consequence of the program. If one family member asks and receives healthier food, it is likely that the other members of the family who previously were not eating healthy food now are.

We used to say that healthy eating begins at home, but these school districts have shown that it can begin at school. Students will eat and even prefer healthy food alternatives whenever healthy foods are made available and unhealthy ones are removed. This is very good news for the health of our children. All school districts should heed this information.

Works Cited

Amato, Rene. *Quantitative Analysis of Student Food Preference Changes*. University of Texas, Aug. 2014 Web. 31 May 2015.

Brinkman, Keith. *Trending Acceptance of Healthy Food by High School Students*. Cornell University, Sept. 2014 Web. 31 May 2015.

Simpson, Rebecca. "Can Student Eating Habits Be Changed Quickly?" *Education Quarterly*. August 2014: 32–40. Print.

Villarreal, Sophia. "The Demand for Healthy Food." *National Review*. 15 May 2014: 45–50. Print.

Whitaker, Marshall. "What's For Lunch?" *Newsweek*. 15 August 2014: 12–16. Print.

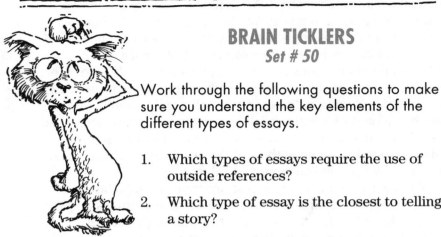

BRAIN TICKLERS
Set # 50

Work through the following questions to make sure you understand the key elements of the different types of essays.

1. Which types of essays require the use of outside references?

2. Which type of essay is the closest to telling a story?

3. Which type of essay requires the most outside research?

4. Which type of essay examines a work of literature?

5. What is the difference between an Argument Essay and an Explanatory Essay?

(Answers are on page 258.)

Edit, edit, edit

Another key to a successful essay is editing, which includes revising and rewriting your essay. Although we don't have space in the book, you should note that each of the example essays would be reviewed, edited, and rewritten as needed. As you edit and rewrite your essay, use the techniques presented earlier in this book to create a quality essay. Pay particular attention to proper transitioning between sentences and proper transitioning between paragraphs. This is where the "E" in POWER comes in. It stands for "Editing." Edit to not only improve the quality of the grammar and sentence structure of your essay, but, more importantly, to also improve your logic and arguments. This is time well spent because your teacher will certainly notice the difference between your essay and one that is thrown together in a single draft.

One final tip: Try not to start every editing session with the first paragraph of your essay. Instead, start your editing with different paragraphs so that each paragraph receives equal treatment when your mind is fresh.

References and citations

Whenever you write a Research Essay or an Argument Essay, you will be required to reference outside sources. Similarly, whenever you write a Literary Analysis Essay, you will be required to cite the literary work itself. The final piece of the template addresses these references (the "R" in POWER). Teachers look for strong references, multiple references, and a variety of references, and they want them to be in proper citation form. A *citation* is an acknowledgment or giving credit to words used by you either in a quote or in a paraphrase from another author or publication in your writing. A *quote* is the use of the exact words of the author, whereas, when you *paraphrase* material, you express the meaning of what the author stated, but you use slightly different words either to clarify the statement or to shorten the statement.

Notice that in both the example Argument Essay and the example Research Essay, we used *parenthetical citations* to alert the reader that we had used an outside reference. These parenthetical citations are short in length so that it doesn't distract the reader from the flow of the essay. At the end of the essay, under "Works Cited," the parenthetical citation is expanded to a full citation to provide the reader the important details of the reference.

I would like to tell you that there is one correct way, and one correct way only, to cite references. Unfortunately, the correct form varies, depending upon the teacher; therefore, pay close attention if your teacher provides you with the format he or she wants for citing references.

If your teacher has not provided you with a format for citing references, the following is the standard Modern Language Association (MLA) format for citing information

- taken from books;
- taken from articles from magazines or journals; and
- taken from Internet sources.

This format can be used for Body Paragraph parenthetical citations and the full citations at the end of the essay under "Works Cited."

Parenthetical Citations

Parenthetical citations should be used only in the body of the essay, and they should be used when you paraphrase an author's work or quote an author's work. If you are paraphrasing a reference, place the parenthetical citation at the end of the sentence containing the paraphrased material. If you are quoting, place the parenthetical citation at the end of the quote. Let's see how to do this.

PROPER PARENTHETICAL CITATION FORM
- *Citing an author from his or her book*
  Write the last name of the author followed by the page you referred to in his or her book. For instance, if you are paraphrasing some information on page 100 from a book by Jane Smith, you would parenthetically cite this as (Smith 100) at the end of the sentence. The period at the end of the sentence follows the closed parenthesis. If you are quoting something on page 100 from Smith, you would insert (Smith 100) after the quote.

- *Citing a source from a printed magazine or journal*
  List the author's last name and page in the magazine or journal on which the reference occurred, e.g., (Smith 100). The citation would occur at the end of a sentence containing paraphrased material or, if you quoted the author, at the end of the quote.
- *Citing an Internet source*
  When taking a reference from an Internet source, you need only write the name of the author, e.g., (Lopez). If the author's name is not provided, then write the name of the web site, e.g., (Healthy Living Today).

After you have inserted you parenthetical citations in the body of your essay, then you will move to the "Works Cited" section at the end of your essay to fully cite your references. Use the format of the following examples to fully cite your references. Notice there are two dates associated with citing an Internet source. The first date is the date of publication of the source itself. The second date is the date that you accessed and used the material.

FULL CITATION FORM

- *Citing a book*
  Landon, Brooks. *Building Great Sentences*. New York: Plume Books, 2013.
- *Citing a magazine or journal article*
  Jones, Margaret, and Sandra Reynolds. "Writing That Term Paper." *Contemporary Writer*, 15 April 2009: 18–25. Print.
- *Citing an Internet source*
  Amato, Rene. *Quantitative Analysis of Student Food Preference Changes*. University of Texas, Aug. 2014 Web. 31 May 2015.

Note: If your entry runs more than one line, indent the second and third lines.

Always list the full citations in alphabetical order according to the author's name. You can refer to the "Works Cited" sections of our Example **Argument Essay** and Example **Research Essay** to see how this is done.

Remember: The above is a guide for you to use if your teacher hasn't provided you with information on how he or she wants you to cite materials in your essay. Always follow your teacher's instructions for citing.

A word about plagiarism

Why do we cite references in the first place? When doing any kind of writing, you must avoid plagiarism. *Plagiarism* is inserting information directly as it is written from a book, magazine article, or web site into your essay without giving credit to its author. When you do this, you give your reader the impression that these particular thoughts or words in your essay are your thoughts or words, rather than those of the author. This is a serious infraction that you must avoid. Many times, teachers will give you a failing grade on your essay for plagiarizing or (if you are lucky) have you rewrite the essay, properly acknowledging your sources. You can use other people's exact words and thoughts, and many times you must in order to give your essay more authority—especially when writing an Argument Essay or a Research Essay. However, to keep yourself from plagiarizing, you need to acknowledge and properly cite your source material.

Practice makes permanent

This chapter's Painless Technique is a simple but powerful one to make writing quality essays easy. Because you do not write essays on a daily basis, it's hard to sharpen this Painless Technique so that it is at your disposal whenever you need it. Therefore, we must look for opportunities to practice it. Try the following, perhaps weekly, to keep this technique fresh in your mind.

1. Using a previous essay, develop a Proposition Statement and an outline for the essay. Do you feel that if you were to write this essay now, it would be better?
2. Practice, and keep practicing, writing the five different types of essays—that way, when you are assigned an essay, it will be second nature to you.

IT'S UP TO YOU!

Make these Painless Techniques from this book an integral part of your writing. Practice them every time you write an essay, a story, or a note on the refrigerator. Within a short amount of time, all of these Painless Techniques will be second nature, and you will be able to confidently write any assignment.

Keep this book at your desk or carry it in your backpack so that if you ever need to review one of the techniques, it will be handy. Good luck and good writing!

BRAIN TICKLERS—THE ANSWERS

Set # 49, page 238

1. Too broad
   <u>Better</u>
   Bicycle riders who wear helmets are 75% less likely to suffer a serious head injury when involved with a collision with a car.

2. Good Proposition Statement

3. Possibly okay
   <u>Better</u>
   I will never again tell my sister a secret, especially when it concerns a girl I like.

4. Too broad
   <u>Better</u>
   The stress of the day seems to melt away during my yoga class.

5. Good Proposition Statement

Set # 50, page 252

1. Argument Essay and Research Essay

2. Narrative Essay

3. Research Essay

4. Literary Analysis Essay

5. Explanatory Essay involves less research and is shorter in length than an Argument Essay.

APPENDIX—FURTHER READING

Aaron, Jane E. *The Little, Brown Compact Handbook*. Sixth edition. New York: Pearson Education, Inc., 2007.

Baugh, L. Sue. *Essentials of English Grammar*. Third edition. New York: McGraw-Hill, 2005.

Beason, Larry and Mark Lester. *Handbook of English Grammar and Usage*. New York: McGraw-Hill, 2005.

The Chicago Manual of Style. Sixteenth edition. Chicago: The University of Chicago Press, 2010.

Elliot, Rebecca. *Painless Grammar*. Third edition. Hauppauge, NY: Barron's Educational Series, 2011.

Gibaldi, Joseph. *MLA Handbook for Writers of Research Papers*. Sixth edition. New York: The Modern Language Association of America, 2002.

Hacker, Diana. *The Bedford Handbook*. Seventh edition. Boston: Bedford/St. Martin's Press, 2006.

Kemper, Dave, Verne Meyer, and Patrick Sebranek. *Writers Inc*. Wilmington, MA: Great Source Education Group, 2001.

MLA Handbook for Writers of Research Papers. Seventh edition. New York: The Modern Language Association of America, 2015.

Paniza, José and Jeffrey Strausser. *Painless English for Speakers of Other Languages*. Hauppauge, NY: Barron's Educational Series, 2007.

Strunk Jr., William and E.B. White. *The Elements of Style*. Third edition. New York: Penguin Books, 2000.

Zinsser, William. *On Writing Well: The Classic Guide to Writing Nonfiction*. Thirtieth edition. New York: Harper Collins Publishers, 2006.

INDEX